W9-BGV-473

THE BEE EATER

MICHELLE RHEE TAKES ON THE NATION'S WORST SCHOOL DISTRICT

RICHARD WHITMIRE

JOSSEY-BASS
A Wiley Imprint
www.josseybass.com

Published by Jossey-Bass
A Wiley Imprint
989 Market Street, San Francisco, CA 94103-1741—www.josseybass.com

Jossey-Bass books and products are available through most bookstores. To contact Jossey-Bass directly call our Customer Care Department within the U.S. at
800-956-7739, outside the U.S. at 317-572-3986, or fax 317-572-4002.

Jossey-Bass also publishes its books in a variety of electronic formats. Some content
that appears in print may not be available in electronic books.

Library of Congress Cataloging-in-Publication Data has been applied for.

ISBN 978-0-470-90529-6
9781118058039 ePDF
9781118058046 eMobi
9781118058053 ePub

Printed in the United States of America
FIRST EDITION
HB Printing   10 9 8 7 6 5 4 3 2 1

CONTENTS

For pretending that single-subject conversations for months in a row are perfectly normal, I thank my lovely wife, Robin.

PREFACE

A grownup might have missed the sign posted at Slowe Elementary in northeast Washington, D.C., but that's beside the point. The sign wasn't put there to catch the attention of adults. It was posted low on the wall, precisely at eye level for the elementary school children moving through the hallways. For those children, the sign was a daily reminder:

> There is nothing a teacher can do to overcome what a parent and a student will not do.

For those children, the sign was a daily admonition that the teachers at Slowe were not responsible for students' failings. We're not the reason the test scores at this school are awful. We're not why D.C. schools rank at the bottom of all the nation's schools. Look to yourself, look to your parents. *You* are to blame.

Michelle Rhee visited Slowe immediately after she was appointed chancellor. It was a day marked by a flurry of school visits, in some cases unannounced. At Slowe, the principal herself unlocked the front door after Rhee and her entourage rang the bell. Her puzzled face gave it away: she had no idea who Rhee was. After introductions, a tour followed, but the visit only got more awkward as the group passed empty classroom after empty classroom. Slowe had been built for hundreds but bizarrely had been allowed to stay open with a mere eighty-three students, a testament to the powerlessness and, in some instances, fecklessness of the parade of superintendents who preceded Rhee (she was the tenth since 1988).

Most of the previous school chiefs had never even considered trying to close schools in the face of a school board and city council inclined to favor an array of special interest groups determined to block any changes to the status quo. Thus, schools such as Slowe were allowed to slog along, year after year, burning up millions of dollars in unneeded maintenance and other inefficiencies. And though it sounds outrageous, that wasn't the saddest part of the story. Conventional wisdom might suggest that with only eighty-three students Slowe Elementary had a shot at being successful. Not so. Similar to the children at D.C.'s many other underused schools, children at Slowe lagged far behind their peers in other cities. At the time Rhee visited Slowe, 35 percent of the students scored at the proficient level in reading and only 15 percent in math.

"The test scores at Slowe were horrible," recalls Tim Daly, Rhee's colleague at The New Teacher Project (a teacher-recruiting organization Rhee helped found), who accompanied Rhee on the tour.[1] It was Daly who noticed the sign in the hallway. Hesitant to trigger a scene during Rhee's first day as chancellor, he didn't tell her until she left the building. "I was thinking, this is the system she has become chancellor of: a system where it would be possible to get appointed chancellor and the principal seemed not to know it, possible for a school built for six hundred students to have fewer than ninety students in it, possible for a school to be failing for years and not get closed, and possible for a teacher to post a sign like that and no one tell the teacher to take it down."

· · · · ·

As Rhee would soon discover, that last point—why no one had demanded the sign be removed—was not the least bit mysterious. It wasn't just one teacher, or one principal, who believed schools had minimal impact on children and therefore were held harmless if students failed to learn. Hundreds of teachers and administrators appeared to have held the same belief. Students in Washington, D.C., they thought, had terrible outcomes because so many came from poor, African American families. In their minds, family formation, race, and poverty added up to destiny. That view had nothing to do with black-white racism; nearly all the teachers, principals, and top administrators were African American. You could have posted that sign in the central office at District of Columbia Public Schools (DCPS), even outside the superintendent's office, and not caused a stir. Even the previous superintendent publicly suggested that was true.[2] In D.C., that's just the way it was, or so they believed.

On a historical level, they were right to believe in the message that families, not schools, were to blame when children failed academically. Judged as a broad data swath, birth's lottery—your zip code, family income, and parental education—does predict destiny with dismaying accuracy. On a comparative level, however, that destiny differs greatly. As the research for this book will demonstrate, other urban school districts with nearly identical demographics held their schools to higher standards and produced far better results.

THE JOB AHEAD

In essence, the D.C. public school system was designed more for adult employment than for teaching and learning. (Think of it as a Department of Public Works that only coincidentally involved schools.) Rhee was assigned the task of transforming those schools in only a few years—which in the school reform world translates to overnight. What happened to Rhee and her team of reformers during the first four years of their crash reforms plays out in the following chapters. The story of her headfirst plunge into dramatic school reform and the equally dramatic tale of the election three-and-a-half years later that forced out both Rhee and Adrian Fenty, the mayor who appointed her, was not the story I expected to find when I began this project. The simple narrative of Rhee versus the teachers' unions portrayed in most of the reporting about Rhee's time in Washington, D.C., is just that: *simple.* In truth, Rhee's clashes were wide ranging and often surprising. They included *The Washington Post* and fellow school reformers who always said they wanted Rhee-style urban school reform but quailed at Rhee's take-no-prisoners method.

And then there's U.S. Secretary of Education Arne Duncan, who handed out millions of dollars of incentive grants trying to lure states into adopting the kind of sophisticated, results-based teacher evaluation system Rhee put into place almost immediately. Somehow, however, Duncan never found the time to stand by her side and show support during her tough times.[3] Rhee, who never flinched when confronting the teachers' unions, was too "hot" for Duncan's team, which sought union cooperation.

Whose style proved more effective? Superficially, it would appear that Duncan's style works better. Unlike Rhee, he still holds his job. But it's far from clear that the reforms inspired by Duncan's collaborative style—the kind where all sides settle on right-sounding reforms while praising the positives of collective bargaining—will produce striking, or even middling, results. Turning around failing urban school districts may require pushing beyond nearly everyone's comfort zone, even Duncan's. Michelle Rhee, however, thrives in that discomfort zone.

Finally, I quickly learned that Rhee's campaign, despite the media focus solely on her, was truly a team effort—an *unusual* team effort. Ever wonder what would happen if a bunch of Teach for America (TFA) rebels with *absolutely no experience* running a school district seized control of one?[4] That's *The Bee Eater* story. This band of reformers couldn't be more different from the usual "big man" approach to radical urban education reform, when a school district taps a retired general (or civilian equivalent) to stiffen the system with his brand of tough love. But failed urban school districts don't need stiffening; they need to be taken apart, given a good scrubbing, and reassembled. These TFAers were willing to take on that task when no one else had the guts. Maybe they had no experience running an urban school district but they did have actual personal experiences succeeding with the kind of urban students whose education they would be overseeing. No general or admiral could claim that kind of experience.

The story behind these radical school reformers coming together as a team under Rhee to fix D.C.'s schools was my impetus for beginning this project. But that story proved to be insignificant compared to what they found waiting for them when they arrived in D.C. and the events that transpired afterward. Everyone knew the Washington, D.C., school system was among the worst in the nation, if not the very worst. But far less was known about *why* the system was so bad. That became apparent in Rhee's first days on the job when she began to tour D.C. schools.

The Race Factor

In Washington, D.C.—a city that attracted thousands of newly freed slaves after the Civil War and then kept them under the thumbs of a seemingly never-ending succession of racist Southern senators who ruled over the District—no story like this is free from discussions of race. Race, from a history of racial persecution to race cards played by D.C. politicians in more recent times, has always been the city's defining identity. Only race can explain why disgraced "mayor for life" Marion Barry remains wildly popular in Anacostia's nearly all-black, impoverished Ward 8. Barry blames "Charlie" (whites) for his constituents' plights; so do many of them. In part, Barry's premise is right. Explaining the plight in Ward 8 starts with this country's history of institutional racism. But the story behind the stall in black academic achievement in D.C. is a little more complicated and includes the patronage system that Barry helped craft, which created a schools system that was more about jobs than student achievement. But in that setup, poor student achievement had to be rationalized. And that's why, prior to Rhee's reforms, Ward 8 schools teemed with teachers and administrators who would have found no fault with the Slowe sign.

What was interesting about Rhee's entanglement with D.C. race issues is how she, at least for a time, disrupted the traditional black-white plot line. Take the story of the turnaround at Anacostia's Sousa Middle School: a Korean American chancellor hires a black principal, who in turn hires black assistant principals. Many black teachers get pushed out or fired, but for the most part they are replaced by new black teachers. Together, this team starts rescuing scores of black children from certain academic failure. The dramatic staff changes at Sousa outraged the Washington Teachers Union. But due to the school's success, and lacking the traditional black-white political framework, the protests proved ineffectual. Think of it as asymmetrical warfare transported to school reform. It took Rhee's critics a full two years to reframe the conflict in more politically convenient terms: Rhee favors whites. Once that storyline was established, Rhee's fate was sealed.

WRITING ABOUT RHEE

Before beginning this book, based on what I had read in the *Post* and teacher-union blogs, I expected to find in Michelle Rhee a personality that would ricochet from fierce to brusque to rude. Isn't that the persona she chose to project when posing for a now-infamous *Time* cover, where she wielded a broom with a no-nonsense glower? "Michelle is someone who will tell you you're wrong and then poke her finger in your eye to make sure you know you're wrong," one person warned me before starting the book project. Just listening to Rhee say that everything she knows about firing people was learned from working for a Toledo, Ohio, sandwich-shop boss named "Grumpy" was enough to convince me that working for Michelle must be intimidating. (I visited Toledo mostly to meet Grumpy [see Chapter One].) But that's not what I experienced with Rhee. I witnessed the fierceness but never saw the rude.

This book is not an authorized biography but Rhee did make herself available for interviews. In the early months Rhee and I fell into a routine: every Wednesday she visited a different school for a "listening session" with teachers—no administrators allowed—to hear gripes, requests for helps, just about anything.

I would show up at her office a half-hour before she departed and then ride along, interviewing during the drive. I came to think of these as the "SUV interviews." Stories about her early childhood in Toledo on the way to the school, stories about high school and college on the way back. If the school was far away and the traffic was bad, all the better from my perspective.

My favorite Michelle story comes from one of those trips. It was late April in Washington, D.C., right before the White House Correspondents Dinner, to which Rhee had been invited. I had been told to meet her forty-five minutes before the listening session, which I found odd, and showed up at the last minute. Bad move. I ran into her charging off the DCPS elevator with a gown on a hanger over her shoulder. "We need to stop at the tailor's," said Rhee. "Come along." A few blocks away we pulled up outside her tailor. I hesitated. Should I give her some personal space and stay in the car? "Come with me, no need to waste any time." So there I was, tagging along, trying my best to thrust my digital recorder somewhere near her lips and ask questions about her childhood as we wove through the crowds. This being Washington, D.C., nobody paid any attention.

On entering the shop Michelle switched to Korean with the tailor. Then she slipped into a bamboo-screened changing area three feet from the front door. This shop was tiny. Assuming she wanted some privacy, I backed out the door. Rhee was having none of that. "It's okay," she said. "Let's continue." So there I was, standing outside this flimsy shield, sticking my recorder through the slats, chatting about her brothers. The Korean tailor found the whole scene hilarious, as did I. But not a moment was wasted and I appreciated that.

One more thing: she looked great in that long ball gown, and with Michelle Rhee appearances matter. People pay attention when a striking woman enters a room. I saw that over and over again when Rhee spoke, unflinching in high heels and perfect outfits that looked like they must have taken days to choose but apparently are snatched up in seconds during high-speed shopping sprints. Fair or not, appearance is power and Rhee was adept at using that power.

FULL DISCLOSURE

Some author biases should be aired here. Rhee wrote the foreword for my previous book, *Why Boys Fail*.[5] I started this book with the gut instinct that Rhee had the best shot in the nation at turning around a failed school district and I ended the book with that instinct mostly intact. Although Chapter Eleven includes a long discussion of Rhee's faults and mistakes, I have no doubt that I will be accused of telling a story favorable to Rhee that ignores the traumas inflicted on the teachers and principals she fired. Fair enough; that's another book waiting to be written. *The Bee Eater* is a narrowly tailored biography, focusing on what made Michelle Rhee into the person who stepped forward to take on the near-impossible task of transforming D.C. schools—and on whether she succeeded.

Midway through gathering data for this book I realized that the significance of what I was watching wasn't Rhee or her band of TFA revolutionaries but rather the power of their antidote to the failures to urban education. Everything I was watching melted down to a principle I'll call *snap*. It's a term I made up, drawing on years of education reporting, my one year of actual classroom teaching (right out of college when I definitely lacked snap), and the months I spent as part of the 2009 Broad Prize for Urban Education evaluation team that visited five of the highest-performing urban school districts in the country. In these high-poverty, high-achieving urban districts, such as Long Beach, California, and Aldine, Texas, nearly all the teachers had snap—a certain quick twitch in their bodies, an urgency in their voices, and a devotion to pursuing a measurable end goal. For *Why Boys Fail* I spent a year keeping track of a boy at one of Washington, D.C.'s best charter schools, KIPP's (Knowledge Is Power Program's) Key Academy. Every teacher I observed there had snap. To teachers with snap, the message of Slowe's hallway sign would make no sense.

Rhee had heard that Slowe message way back when she was a novice teacher in Baltimore—and rejected it. Her plan to introduce a new generation of teachers with snap to D.C. was, to use Michelle's favorite word, *crazy*. She uses it to describe nearly everything. It's *crazy* when she finds a principal who hides out in the office all day (and needs to be fired). It's *crazy* when she discovers union contracts that force her to find positions for ineffective teachers who were pushed out of their previous school for being bad teachers. During one of our interviews I asked her to define *crazy*, and she laughed. "Maybe we use that word too much." Maybe not.

As the track record will show, both in the District of Columbia and nationally, it takes a crazy person to produce results under the conditions Rhee faced. Ultimately, *The Bee Eater* is the story of a crazy woman taking on a crazy school system. It's also about what it actually takes to achieve what Arne Duncan, corporate leaders, and just about everyone else agrees is not only the *right* goal but also the necessary goal for the future of our country: to give all children, not just those in the suburbs, a crack at the American Dream.

ACKNOWLEDGMENTS

Several years ago when serving as president of the National Education Writers Association I played a role in creating the position of "public editor" for the organization, someone who could help education reporters cope with the dwindling education expertise at their own publications by providing assistance ranging from sources to editing. Little did I know then that one day I would be leaning on that public editor, author and former *Washington Post* education reporter Linda Perlstein. She combed through every word of every chapter and made me look like a better writer.

Andrew Rotherham of Eduwonk and Bellwether fame helped me make sure I got the "big picture" of Rhee's role in the education reform movement right. The person who knows everything there is to know about the history of (mostly failed) education reform efforts in Washington, D.C., Mike Casserly from the Council of Great City Schools, steered me back in the right direction several times. Kati Haycock from The Education Trust did the same.

This book could never have come together so quickly without grants from the Broad and Kauffman foundations. A special thanks to Erica Lepping at Broad and Ben Wildavsky and Margo Quiriconi at Kauffman. These grants paid for interview transcriptions, a researcher (nice work, Jonathan

Mills from the University of Arkansas), and for the services of Clarus Research, which I hired to poll families around a particular middle school in the Anacostia neighborhood of Washington, D.C. Accepting a grant from Broad, one of the funders contributing to D.C.'s pay-for-performance program, may strike some as a potential conflict. In truth, neither Broad nor Kauffman asked for any input on the book. In fact, they never even saw *The Bee Eater* until it was published. Joe Williams from Democrats for Education Reform volunteered to act as the "pass through" for the grants without taking a cent for his efforts, which allowed me to invest everything in book research.

I first got to know Michelle Rhee through my role as president of the National Education Writers Association. She was a frequent speaker at our events. Later, I asked Rhee to write the foreword to my last book, *Why Boys Fail*, and was impressed by the thought and effort that went into her piece. Soon after the boys book was published I began thinking about my next project. If I wrote another book, I wanted it to have a natural narrative. Who did I know in the education world with a compelling life narrative? One person came immediately to mind. It took a month or so to talk Rhee into cooperating (at least partly) for a book, but eventually she agreed. *The Bee Eater* is not an authorized biography but Rhee gave me enough access (and a green light to talk to friends, family, and former work associates) to enable me to research and write the book.

Rhee's parents, Shang and Inza, who were generous with their time and memories, supplied the family photographs seen in the book. And I need to thank Michelle for opening up (cautiously at first, granted) about her reform efforts in D.C. Considering how often she had gotten burned by national publicity, that could not have been an easy decision for her.

Within Rhee's staff, I leaned on Jason Kamras for contract and teacher-quality questions, Kaya Henderson for the big picture, Abigail Smith for political history and school closings, Lisa Ruda for policy history, and Erin McGoldrick for data questions. Also helpful was Richard Nyankori, who carried out an epic and mostly thankless struggle to regain control of the district's monstrous special education dilemma.

In the D.C. schools, I am grateful for the time and access Dwan Jordon at Sousa Middle School gave me. I wish I could have been there November 5, 2010, when he took his entire school to see *Waiting For "Superman."* In the movie, Sousa was the school "Anthony" desperately needed to avoid—the "sinkhole" of D.C. schools. At the time the movie was shot, getting sent to Sousa meant certain academic death. Thanks to Rhee and Jordon, however, that's no longer the case.

I want to thank George Leonard and his entire Friends of Bedford team at Dunbar High School for their time. As for the numerous principals who granted me access . . . thanks. Sometimes education writers have to see schools they know they won't be profiling in a book. Also, I want to thank all of the people who spoke to me on and off the record for this book. I know how valuable your time was and so appreciated your sharing your insights and stories with me.

Among those I interviewed from Rhee's pre-D.C. life, a special thanks to Tim Daly, president of The New Teachers Project. Daly is in the unique position of knowing Rhee's life both before and after she came to D.C. As the interview transcribers will attest, Daly talks really, really fast. Those interviews cost me double!

To our daughters, Morgan and Tyler, thanks for putting up with all my nervous energy while working on the book. And a special thanks to Tyler for helping shape that chapter on teacher quality, something she learned about through her work in Oregon for Stand for Children. To my parents, Blanton and Peg, your inspiration and support will never be forgotten. To my wife, Robin, the dedication page says it all.

My book agents, Howard Yoon and Gail Ross, helped guide this project from beginning to end. And finally, my editor at Jossey-Bass, Lesley Iura, kept everything calm as we pushed up the publication date by eight months to meet the reality of Rhee's departure. Yes, you heard that right: eight months. What's striking about Iura and the entire team at Jossey-Bass is that they absorbed most of the eight months while protecting my writing time. Very classy bunch there, which also includes Leslie Tilley, Amy Reed, Dimi Berkner, Pamela Berkman, and Samantha Rubenstein.

INTRODUCTION

T he usually cool October weather in Baltimore was absent that day in 1992. It was hot, especially inside the cinderblock classroom overseen by twenty-one-year-old rookie teacher Michelle Rhee at Harlem Park Elementary. The school was located in a neighborhood so seedy that it was used in "The Wire," HBO's acclaimed series about the relentless, and mostly fruitless, police campaign against drug traffickers in West Baltimore. (A decade after Rhee left Harlem Park, the television crew would use the school's parking lots for their vans, the gym for storing gear, and the streets where Rhee's students lived for their real-world drug culture.) Most homes were boarded up; every other street corner sprouted young men with no future. This was before the crack epidemic abated; many of the parents with children in Harlem Park were users. When kids showed up for school disheveled, cared for only by an older child, the principal didn't need to ask why.

"These kids were having a lot of home problems," said Linda Carter, Harlem Park's principal during Rhee's second and third years there. "Some of them actually had to sleep under the bed because of the shootings that occurred every night. Kids might not see their mother for days and then, walking to school, see their mother high on the corner. It was just that kind of area. Before school dismissal, I would go out into the streets with some of the male teachers and clear an area, making sure no drug transactions were going on."

Carter remembers a neighborhood "summit" she organized that drew some of the movers and shakers behind the drug trade. Her goal was to stop the dealers on the small-tire bikes who would show up when the adjoining middle school was dismissed and strew drugs on the ground as a temptation. "Everyone would scatter (for the drugs) like cockroaches," said Carter.

That October day, Rhee, fresh from a sheltered academic life at Cornell University and beginning a two-year commitment with Teach for America, was fighting for control over her class of thirty-six second-graders. And also fighting for her dignity. For Rhee, the daughter of a physician who grew up in a placid neighborhood in Toledo, raised to always be the best at what she did, this was her first flirtation with failure. And this was no transient failure. On some days that school year, when Michelle would wake up and realize it was another school day, her stomach churned and her body broke out in hives.

On this day, even more than most, absolutely nothing was going right. Rhee had stayed up late the night before making a graphically attractive lesson. She had constructed elaborate props using construction paper and marshmallows and carefully taped tiny magnets to the back of each. The plan: use the marshmallows as hands-on learning tools for a lesson on adding and subtracting. "I had brought in marshmallows for the kids to eat. That was my big bribe." But the first marshmallow slid down the blackboard. Unlike nearly all school blackboards, it turned out, this blackboard was not magnetized. It was at that very low point, when nobody in the class was listening, nobody was sitting still, nobody cared about construction-paper marshmallows, nobody cared about math, that Rhee looked to some relief from both the heat and her out-of-control class. She opened a window and in flew a big, fat bumblebee.

"Literally, the kids started going nuts," she recalled. "A bee! A bee! A bee! They were running around the room, jumping on the chairs. It was 100 percent chaos. I was trying to settle them down when the bee landed near the air vent, right by the window. I had my rolled-up lesson plan about the marshmallows, which was now no good, and I smacked the bee and then flipped it into my hand—and ate it. It wasn't that bad. I didn't chew. I couldn't feel it moving in my mouth. I just swallowed."

Suddenly, the class drew silent in amazement. For the first time, they realized that their teacher, this diminutive young Korean woman lacking any powers of intimidation, might just be crazy, someone deserving of respect. Swallowing the bee that day didn't solve Rhee's discipline problems. That breakthrough was still months away. But after that day, the students afforded her just a bit of deference, just as they would any potentially crazy person on the street corner.

That evening, carpooling home with Liz Peterson, a roommate who was a Teach for America teacher in a nearby school, Rhee mentioned the fact that she ate a bumblebee that day. Neither thought it was strange. Both were struggling, seeing crazy things, doing crazy things. Said fellow Baltimore TFAer Roger Schulman, "Everything was so insane for her and all of us that first year. The normal boundaries of what one would do just flew out the window. We did whatever we had to do."

• • • • •

Adrian Fenty, who would appoint Michelle Rhee schools chancellor shortly after taking office in 2007, spent the six years he served on the Washington, D.C., city council (2000–2006) watching a stream of school super-intendents pass through the nation's capital. Some fled quickly; they never stood a chance against the naysayers opposing change. School board members, councilmembers, the mayor, the Washington Teachers Union, the special education lawyers, self-styled education "experts" wield-ing agendas: it was a long list. Others stayed for a sliver of time before moving on; none wrested any real change in the school system that by any measure rivaled Los Angeles for worst-in-the-nation status. Oddly, to many D.C. resi-dents the schools situation seemed acceptable. The District of Columbia Public Schools had proved to be a bountiful employer; the central office alone teemed with hundreds of unneeded workers taking home paychecks but contribut-ing little or nothing to classroom achievement. The dismal academic standings? Conventional wisdom—including, it seemed, at *The Washington Post*—held that race and poverty, not ineffective teaching, explained that embarrassment. Occasionally, the newspaper launched an impressive series on D.C. school boilers not working, a baffling inability to count the number of students within its own system, or teachers absconding with student activities money. But the important issue—whether and why academic achievement in D.C. lagged well behind cities with similar student populations—was rarely explored.

And because some parents had options besides DCPS's failing schools, the system was let off the hook. Independent charter schools pulled in a rapidly growing number of families; others could apply for "out-of-boundary" schools in better-off neighborhoods. That produced happier parents but only because few were aware that the nicer schools, often dominated by out-of-boundary students from the poorest neighborhoods, were failing, too. Worse, although the out-of-boundary strategy relieved political stress it created two academic landmines. First, it was hard to get parents involved with school activities and conferences when they lived so far away. Second, and far more important, the lack of a district-wide K–12 curriculum truly let down students who scattered to one neighborhood for elementary school, another for middle school, and who-knows-where for high school.[1] In truth, DCPS was a barely breathing school system, impervious to reform. From the sidelines of the council, Fenty, a Howard University–trained lawyer who grew up in the city, witnessed it all. "I had seen really good people come through the school board and have almost no positive impact," he said. "It was all for the same reason: because there was an inability to make tough decisions. Any tough decision that was proposed, no matter who proposed it, would never get the majority of people to support it. . . . The special interests would come out and it would die a quick death."

It wasn't that Fenty felt he had all the answers; it's more that he had instincts about which direction to head in, should he be elected mayor. He had watched Mayor Michael Bloomberg take control of the schools in New York City and Mayor Richard Daley do so in Chicago. "The more I got to know about what they had done, both about the substantive changes they could make in education and the general positive impact that had on the city, I became more and more convinced that D.C. needed to follow suit," said Fenty, who took office on January 2, 2007. That meant not just seizing control of the schools but also finding a "change agent" like Joel Klein, the former federal prosecutor whom Bloomberg tapped to run the city schools. Klein, an unconventional choice, moved the city's academic indicators upward only by shredding common thinking about how to run an urban school district, such as placing charter schools inside traditional schools, imposing test-based school evaluation systems, taking on teacher work rules deemed sacred by the teachers union, and trying to fire ineffective teachers. To push D.C. toward becoming a world-class city, Fenty needed his own change agent, someone willing to step on toes daily, maybe even hourly, and turn a deaf ear to squeals. Adrian Fenty needed a bee eater.

Chapter One

AN (ASIAN) AMERICAN LIFE

Onething many people want to know about Michelle Rhee is who raised this firebrand? The question is understandable. Among Korean immigrants, the appetite for controversial public encounters is nonexistent. Usually, first-generation children of Korean immigrants seek first-class college degrees and settle into quiet suburban lives as doctors and engineers. Yet here we have Michelle Rhee, whose plunge into running D.C. schools generated so much controversy that it landed her on the cover of *Time* and spawned a twelve-part, three-year television documentary on PBS. In the news, we would see dramatic images of a Korean American female facing down the opposition, usually very angry African Americans at least two or three heads taller and a hundred pounds heavier. And yet she never blinked. Again: who raised her?

MICHELLE'S ROOTS

One day in late spring 2010, Michelle's parents, father Shang and mother Inza, sat side by side on a smallish sofa next to me at her Washington, D.C., home off 16th Street near the Rock Creek Park Tennis Center. They were midway through one of their many visits to Washington, D.C., from their Colorado retirement home to help care for their granddaughters, Starr and Olivia. What was odd to me was the dynamic between the two of them: Inza, everyone assured me, is the firebrand, the fierce one from whom Rhee inherited her obliviousness to political pain. Yet when I asked about family history, Inza smiled and deferred to Shang, a retired physician, to handle the initial response. Don't be fooled, Michelle cautioned me afterward. Her mother merely was not 100 percent confident speaking in English, especially in an interview. She was nervous she would say the wrong thing. Usually, that's not how they operate. Usually, Inza runs the show.

True enough, the parents agree. Even though Shang does most of the talking during interviews in English, Inza is the steely one, and says she gets it from her father, who "had fire." She is one of six children born to a police officer who later ran a municipal entertainment center and an old-fashioned Korean mother who stayed at home to take care of the children. Inza married Shang and in 1965 they moved to the United States so that he could attend medical school at the University of Michigan, where Michelle was born on Christmas Day, 1969. Then they moved to Rossford, a suburb of Toledo, so that Shang could pursue his specialty of pain management. Inza became a Western-style entrepreneur and opened an upscale dress shop.

Inside their suburban home in Toledo, Inza exercised exacting Korean-style control. She wanted to raise Michelle the way she was raised. She famously sewed her daughter into her prom dress to erase even a suggestion of décolletage (and later used scissors to get her out), grounded Michelle when her distracted brother Brian faltered in school, because that meant she hadn't helped him enough, and, according to a family friend, dropped Michelle off at Cornell with the parting words, "We didn't bring you to Cornell to get an Ivy League education; we brought you here to find an Ivy League husband."

"My mother was very strict," Inza says. "She didn't let me do anything but study. She didn't let me go to the movies or anything. Just study." Inza's rule-making with Michelle, however, was an East-West cross—Korean tradition melded into a Western "out there" flair arising from her successful business career. It was a potent combination that triggered growing-up traumas for Michelle.

"It's funny because none of my cousins who ended up growing up in Korea were raised that way because in Korea things were changing," said Michelle, who has an older and a younger brother.[1] Her parents, she said, were in a "time warp. I was only allowed out in the evening one night a week and had to be back by 11 p.m. My brothers, however, could do whatever they wanted." Today, Inza laughs at her daughter's memories of the family's double standards. "I'm a Korean mother," she said. "Korean moms are always stricter on girls than boys."

As for sewing up the front and back of Michelle's prom dress while she was in it, Inza did it because it was too low-cut for her liking: "She could wear it or stay home." Then Inza chuckles and adds, "She complained a lot when she was little." Regardless, the childhood tensions appear to have abated and today both would agree with Michelle's observation: "My mom was very strong-willed. I inherited a ton of the way I am from her."

Shang, by contrast, has been the even-tempered intellectual of the family. He reads deeply about science and medicine and has a great sense of humor. Growing up, everyone loved Dr. Rhee, from Michelle's friends to those who worked with him at the hospital. Although Shang and Inza may sound like the classic odd couple, it's obvious they are close. He pursues his intellectual passions while she whirls away taking care of family business. "One time," recalled Michelle, "my dad was sitting on the couch reading the newspaper with the television on. At the same time my mother was buzzing around the house doing fifty million things. Suddenly, she picks up a can of Rogaine and sprays it on his head. And he's sitting there, not moving, while she sprays the Rogaine on him."

· · · · ·

For elementary school, Michelle attended a neighborhood public school, Eagle Point Elementary—"the most vanilla public school you could ever imagine," Michelle said. The family lived in a well-off neighborhood in Rossford, an otherwise working-class city. Today, a drive around Rossford could be included in a documentary about the radical decline of America's manufacturing prowess. The skeletons of hulking factories surrounded by empty parking lots serve as brutal reminders of an economic base that isn't returning. A small sliver of Rossford, however, borders the wide and lazy Maumee River just before it flows into the Maumee Bay of Lake Erie. That neighborhood, entered through stone portals that set it off from the rest of Rossford, is slung close the river. It's the kind of leafy neighborhood, dotted with large, expensive homes where one would expect a successful physician to live with his family. When I visited the neighborhood, the only people seen on the winding streets were the lawn care workers. The Rhees lived at 261 Riverside Drive until the house burned down a few years ago, Inza and Shang narrowly escaping.

After sixth grade, Michelle followed the family tradition of spending a year in Korea, where she stayed with her aunt and cousin who was a year younger. Every day, she went to school with her cousin. In Ohio, Michelle was the only Korean in her class. In Korea, she was the odd one out again: her Korean vocabulary amounted to what she could absorb at the family dinner table. "It was a tough experience," she said. "The school environment there is so different. There were seventy to seventy-five students per class. We all sat in these little rows and were seated according to height. Since I was taller, I sat in the back with another tall girl. Nobody spoke English, so I just sat there and tried to pick up what I could, but I really didn't understand 90 percent of what was going on."

Rhee's parents and Michelle would agree that the year in Korea was formative. "One thing she learned was closeness of extended family members," Shang said. "I think that was striking to her." Inza agrees that her daughter returned a different person. "Until then, she knew how to read and write Korean, because we sent her to Korean school, but she didn't really speak Korean that well. So she went to elementary school and she had to work really hard. She changed a lot."

· · · · ·

After Michelle returned, Shang and Inza ratcheted up the academic pressure by sending her to Maumee Valley Country Day School, an independent school in Toledo where she followed in the footsteps of her older brother, Erik. Maumee

Valley was the only elite private school in Toledo. Set on seventy-five wooded acres broken up by playing fields and carefully designed academic buildings, all intended to meld into the woods, the 125-year-old school enrolls fewer than five hundred students for grades three through twelve. The tuition, $16,000 in 2010, is modest for this kind of independent school but by far the highest private school tuition in Toledo. The school enrolls many of the sons and daughters from the University of Toledo Medical Center, Bowling Green State University, and University of Toledo. The students are drawn from a city that since the 1990s has been slammed by the implosion of manufacturing. When Maumee Valley graduates go away to college, and all do, they rarely return to Toledo to take jobs and raise a family. "When I do alumni visits, I go up and down the East Coast, up and down the West Coast," said head of school Gary Boehm.

At Maumee Valley, Rhee established herself not as an academic star but as the master organizer. "I was the person who ran everything," she said. "I was not the queen bee or most popular student but I knew who was doing what with whom and I would coordinate everything. I was student council president and all that stuff. I was very well-rounded. I played sports and was the captain of a bunch of teams. I wasn't necessarily the best player. I was more of a leader."

Pete Chung hailed from another Korean American family in Rossford, just down the street. Together, the Rhees and Chungs accounted for the entire Korean American presence in the area. Pete and Michelle became close friends and what Pete, now a venture capitalist in San Francisco, recalls about Michelle is her unflappability and imperviousness to peer pressures. Pete admits to being the typical teenager—fretting about what people thought of him, trying to act cool. Michelle, by contrast, went her own way. At the end of seventh grade, Pete and Michelle, who were in the same grade together, won permission from the Chung parents to throw an end-of-school-year party. Enormous planning went into the party, especially the guest list. The party was a huge hit, but afterward the Maumee Valley students who didn't get invited were upset and determined to take revenge. "I started getting nasty crank calls," recalled Pete, who became really worried about the fallout and called Michelle to warn her of imminent consequences. Her response: "Ah, screw 'em."

That independent streak extended into the high school years, when Michelle did things many other students would never do, such as carve out close personal relationships with faculty members. Traditional teenage rebelliousness—drinking, smoking, cursing—wasn't a part of Michelle's life. One of her closest friends is Gretchen Verner. In high school, the two of them would go to parties and leave five minutes later when it became clear drinking was the whole purpose of the party.

Twice, they violated their anti-drinking instincts. Neither time turned out well. The first time they decided they needed to vent their anger that much of the senior field hockey team couldn't start the season opener because they had been caught drinking. Marshalling some kind of shaky teenage logic, they decided to seek revenge by drinking themselves. "I made her a rum and Coke," Gretchen recalled. It didn't go well. "Michelle turned bright red." The second encounter with alcohol happened their senior year when Gretchen and Michelle learned they didn't get into their first-choice colleges: Yale for Gretchen, Princeton for Michelle. Now was the time for a traditional high school protest response, they concluded: let's drink. Problem was, at Michelle's house all they found was a dusty old bottle of Kahlua. Her parents aren't drinkers either. Regardless, they indulged. Again, it didn't turn out well for Michelle and it didn't take that much Kahlua to find out.

Today, Michelle laughs about those memories. "I learned early on that I don't have the tolerance for alcohol," she said. "Some Koreans don't have the enzyme that digests alcohol, so it goes straight to you, even if you take just one sip." As she pointed out, not drinking allows her to keep a demanding schedule that extends well into the night. As D.C. schools chancellor she didn't even begin her treadmill work-out until 10 p.m. As for smoking, that experiment didn't last long either. Once, Michelle decided she needed to rebel against her mother, Gretchen recalled, so they bought a pack of cigarettes, drove to the mall where her mother's store was located and smoked. That protest was also short lived.

THE WIDER WORLD

Michelle repeatedly befriended people unlike her. The first was Jewel Woods. Each year Maumee Valley reached into Toledo's schools and plucked one or two promising minority students. Most of the African American students selected were middle-class blacks. Not Woods, who by his own description was pure street, raised by his grandmother after age eight because of his mother's drug problems. Before applying to Maumee Valley County Day School, he had already dropped out of his public school in Toledo. But through friends Woods had heard about the scholarship openings at the private school and something—to this day he doesn't know what, perhaps some previously concealed intellectual curiosity—prompted him to apply. His test scores were lousy and his entrance essay was poorly written. But something compelling about the ambition of his essay, "Why black students were never pushed to achieve," and something attractive about his curiosity got him admitted.

Getting admitted, however, was not the same as surviving. "I was a fish out of water," he said. "I had a Jheri curl and a broken front tooth." With a small class, there was no hiding in the back. A poor student with a fear of public speaking and slight stutter, Woods was an unlikely candidate to be befriended by the hyper confident, socially adept Michelle Rhee. And yet he was. The friendship—which included a period of dating—even survived into the third year, when Woods returned to the private school a "militant," the result of attending a summer program for young black achievers. Part of that summer session included a public speaking course, which prepared him to deliver a scorcher of a speech on the opening day of his junior year, a time when students are invited to speak about their summer. Woods delivered a "jaw-dropping" speech about race and class that nobody knew how to deal with; only Michelle remained his friend. "What makes Michelle unique is that for some unbeknownst reason, she's always had the quality of being an old spirit in a young person's body," Woods said. "Michelle was always the person people took their problems to. She always had that quality where she was comfortable with diversity and felt willing to explore race and class."

During his time at the school Woods occasionally accepted rides home from other students. But he never had them drop him off at his actual house, where he lived with his grandmother. It was too embarrassing. "I'd have them drop me off two or three blocks from my house and then I'd walk home. Michelle Rhee was the only person I ever brought to my house, and she didn't blink." To Rhee, seeing where Woods lived on the west side of Toledo was startling, a universe apart from where Michelle lived on Riverside Drive. "I had never seen anything like it," she said. Today, Woods runs an Ohio-based nonprofit that focuses on men's issues. He and Rhee have maintained their friendship over the years.

Rhee was friends with most of the other African Americans at Maumee Valley, too—something she attributes to being an outsider of sorts herself, the only Korean American student in her 1988 graduating class of fifty-one students. "I lived a very odd life," she said. "I was very much in the mix with rich, white, established people. But I also had a wide range of friends." That mix can be glimpsed in Rhee's senior page, the full yearbook page private schools usually devote to each graduating senior. Rhee's senior page was a weave of old world and new world. The upper left corner is devoted to photos of her female relatives from Korea, including her mother and grandmother. The photo is offset, however, with a hipster caption: "What is this? The Ms. Korea pageant?" There's a photo of a chubby-cheeked Michelle sitting on the hood of a car with her brothers that carries the caption: "Brian and Erik—the two best brothers I could ask for. Thanks for being my friends." The photo at the bottom right shows five boys from her graduating class, most looking highly preppy and bristling with attitude in their jeans, sneakers, ties, and sport coats. They, too, were a part of her world.

Rhee's high school boyfriend, Adam Weiss, was another unlikely choice. Weiss tended toward the sullen side, a sharp contrast to the outgoing Rhee. Over time, the relationship that had a huge impact on Rhee was with Adam's mother, Mary, who taught at the Martin Luther King, Jr. Elementary School in Toledo, an inner-city school that was another world apart from Maumee Valley. "She and Adam came to my school one afternoon and Michelle thought it was great," said Weiss. "She came back without Adam to volunteer. She absolutely adored the kids and would read with them. She became a regular." The friendship with Mary kept blossoming, prompted in part by the fact that Adam's sister had died at the age of ten. Michelle, in some ways, became the missing daughter, a regular in the Weiss household. "Adam wasn't much of a talker and Michelle and I would just talk," Weiss said. "I loved it. She was part of the family and she never left." To Rhee, the Weisses were the "idyllic American family," a refreshing contrast to what she viewed as her own overly strict household. Rhee said that volunteer work at Martin Luther King, Jr., along with a summer working with kids on an Indian reservation in Saskatchewan, Canada, explain how she got to where she is today.

· · · · ·

Michelle spent several summers working at Grumpy's, a Toledo sandwich shop. Jeff Horn was born into the hardware business, a job he says made him grumpy. So in the early 1980s he began converting hardware space into a sandwich shop, which he named Grumpy's. In 1986, when a panda exhibit came to the Toledo Zoo, Horn decided to open a Grumpy's annex across the street to feed the crowds. Rhee was one of several high school students he hired and, during the course of that summer, the only one he didn't fire. "He wasn't called Grumpy for no reason," Michelle said. "He would scream and yell all the time. And fire people all the time. Somebody new would get hired and we would guess how long he or she would last. What I learned from him was that if it's not working out, just fire the person. Be clear with the person and take care of it right away."

During my visit to Grumpy's in summer 2010, I found a far mellower Jeff Horn working the cash register at a nicely appointed lunch restaurant in downtown Toledo, just a short walk from Fifth Third Field, the stadium to the minor league baseball team, the Toledo Mud Hens. He was wearing a tie— "I never saw him wear a tie," said Rhee when I told her about my visit and that Jeff laughed about memories of Rhee. "I never saw that man laugh," she claims, but that's likely shtick. Jeff and his wife, Connie, who worked in the business as a partner, came to Rhee's first wedding.

The part about firing workers, however, is plenty real. In the restaurant business, explained Horn, you go through a lot of workers. "Not all people are created equal," he said. "There are certain jobs you can't put up with inefficiencies. When someone doesn't work out, they're not going to get any better. There isn't any easy way to do it. You cut bait and get it over with." He told Michelle, "You're never going to make a Stradivarius out of knotty pine, so when you want a Stradivarius, get rid of the knotty pine." Horn said Rhee was a "peach" of a worker, a master of multitasking. "She was a machine. Tell her to go and she'd go. You didn't have to manage Michelle."

Restaurant work became a routine for Rhee. In college at Cornell, in Ithaca, New York, she worked for a Japanese res-taurant. "I probably spent more time working than I should have," said Rhee. "I paid for my own living expenses; my parents paid the tuition. I think waiting tables is one of the best things people can do for just general life skills because you have to be with it, you have to learn how to manage."

Years later, when Rhee was married to Kevin Huffman and their daughters were small, the family entered an Original Pancake House restaurant in Toledo. "There's always a wait there," said Huffman. "This time it was a forty-five-minute wait, so they're taking names, but all the people working there were kind of milling around and there were open tables. All the other customers were complaining. At first, Michelle goes over and peeks over the podium to look at the wait list. Then she's sort of looking everything over and wandering around the restaurant. Then she takes over the podium and says to the staff there, 'You, take this family and put them at the four-top there. You, take these guys to the two-top.' They were all following her orders. She cleaned out the backlog in about five minutes. Everyone's seated! It was the funniest damn thing. And the hilarious thing was that the restaurant workers listened. They were like, 'Now here's someone with a plan.'"

·····

When it came to applying to colleges, Rhee had every extracurricular imaginable and very good grades. But she got turned down by every Ivy League college to which she applied. "See, I'm not book-smart," she said. "I didn't really do great on the SATs. I was in a class of fifty kids, which is not a lot, and they were some of the smartest kids in Toledo. I was always trying to make it to the top 20 percent. Some semesters I'd make it, some I wouldn't." At one point, after losing out at the Ivies, Rhee was leaning toward Miami University of Ohio, which had offered her a scholarship. "It was my thought that if I was going to go somewhere I didn't want to go, I might as well go for free . . . and my parents said absolutely not." So she went to the more prestigious Wellesley College. Although Rhee's mother is usually the forceful one, in this case it was Shang who stepped in firmly. "I didn't push her to do that [go to Wellesley] but I encouraged her to think bigger." Shang Rhee, who graduated from the prestigious Seoul National University, believed that deepened his aspirations in life and wanted his daughter to experience the same. After one year at Wellesley, Rhee transferred to Cornell University. She was finally in the Ivy League.

At Cornell, her roommate was fellow transfer student Melissa Williams-Gurian. "What's interesting about Michelle is she's hard to read and at least initially, not very warm and fuzzy," Williams-Gurian said. "I remember calling my father and saying my roommate is fine, but I don't think we're going to be friends. But that's just part of who Michelle is. She has a strong exterior and does not allow everyone in. But once in, she's this loving, generous, loyal friend." When Williams-Gurian's father remarried, an event that wasn't going to be easy for her, Rhee showed up to support her friend. "I was like, 'Wow, you're really going to come?'"

One of the first things Williams-Gurian noticed about Rhee was the same thing everyone comments on: she loves nice clothes. In her senior year of high school Rhee was voted "best-dressed." The usual college uniform, jeans and sneakers, weren't her style. "Michelle's closet was full; you can't imagine how full," Williams-Gurian said. "I rarely saw the same outfit twice." Friends from every stage of Michelle's life recall her distinctive look, fashionable but not enslaved to fashion. "She had this incredible closet," said high school friend Gretchen Verner.

"She would have outfits for different seasons and rotate them into her closet," raiding her mother's stash when need be, too. Her friends assumed all those clothes came from her mother's shop because they couldn't recall Rhee ever venturing out to go shopping. She did, but not in the way many women did. "I'm not a shopper in the usual sense of the word," Michelle said. "My mother will go to a place like T.J.Maxx all day and look at everything. I can't do that. I go in and know what I like and am very decisive. If I get the right salesperson, they hit the goldmine. I will buy a ton of stuff all at once and go on." Her current favorite: Nordstrom. Loves the customer service.

· · · · ·

With hindsight, it may strike some as odd that Rhee's initial attraction to Cornell, dating back to her senior year of high school, was the hotel management school there. She had applied but didn't get in. When Rhee transferred to Cornell, she thought she could transfer into the hotel program but her interests soon shifted, due in part to joining a group called Peer Educators in Human Relations. "We would go out and train students how to be more sensitive to diversity," she said. "That was my radical Asian phase. I grew up totally assimilated, essentially thinking I was white. I grew up around white people. That was all I knew. Then when I went to Cornell, I was around lots of other Asian people and other ethnic groups. That is when I sort of noticed who I was." Williams-Gurian recalls long discussions with Rhee comparing their own privileged lives to those less fortunate. "She went through a period of not dating white men."

Rhee ended up majoring in government but when her senior year arrived she had no idea what she wanted to do.

Then she saw a PBS documentary on Teach for America. "I thought it was the greatest thing I had ever seen," she said. "They showed four TFA corps members going through their first year of teaching. It was sad because one of them was really bad and got fired on national TV. And there was the Korean guy who taught science. You could tell he was a great teacher and I thought, 'This is great.'" Rhee went to the information session and then applied. Her sample teaching lesson: how to say *hello* in Japanese, both formally and informally. It must have gone well; she was accepted.

· · · · ·

Everyone who knows Michelle Rhee agrees that a core set of influences answer the question of where this unique person came from. Everything started with Inza's iron will and the compliance and rebellion that triggered, combined with Shang's urges toward community service. In Seoul, surviving in a challenging environment gave her a measure of steel. Volunteering in Mary Weiss's urban Toledo classroom planted in Rhee a possible future. And the "radical Asian phase" at Cornell pushed her to embrace the ambitious and bold. By her senior year in college, the personality of the woman seen trying to transform D.C. public schools was already well formed.

Verner, one of Michelle's oldest friends, has seen Michelle cry only twice. The first was when Gretchen accompanied Michelle to Korea to visit her relatives when they were both twenty. Michelle had become very close to her grandmother and in the cab to the airport for the return trip, Verner looked over and saw tears rolling down her friend's cheeks. They didn't need to speak for Verner to know that Rhee thought it might be the last time she would see her grandmother.

The second time she saw Michelle cry was on her wedding day in 1996, when, according to Korean custom, Inza gathered all the cash wedding gifts and claimed them as contributions toward the parents' wedding expenditures. That's how it's done in Korea but not in the United States—hence the tears. In years to come, during the worst travails as a newbie teacher in one of Baltimore's most depressing neighborhoods, the stresses of life triggered hives but no tears. A bee eater in the making.

Chapter Two

THE TRANSFORMATION BEGINS

A year earlier back at Cornell, when Rhee first heard of Teach for America on TV, she never could have imagined it would come to this. It's not like she had ever eaten insects. It's not like she had ever broken out in stress welts. In truth, she had never failed at anything in life, only excelled. Sitting in a dorm room in Cornell watching that PBS segment, this seemed like the perfect next chapter in her life, a perfect chance for more success. "In college I had no idea what I wanted to do," she said. "I've never been a person who knew exactly where she wanted to go. Then I saw that documentary on Teach for America, and I thought it was really cool."

Rhee had also been accepted into a graduate program in industrial and labor relations and called her eighty-year-old grandmother in Korea to solicit advice about which path to pursue. The advice: "Go be a teacher."

"Yeah, but it's going to be really hard," Rhee replied and tried to explain the challenges endured by Teach for America candidates. "They're little kids," her grandma replied. "What's hard about that?" Rhee's parents were less enthusiastic. Their attitude: "We sent you to Cornell and spent all that money so you could teach poor kids?"

Rhee chose Teach for America and joined the rest of the TFAers for summer training at California State University's Northridge campus in Los Angeles. Wake up at 5 a.m., get on a bus at 6 a.m., suffer through L.A.'s traffic to get dropped off at an elementary school for classroom observations and practice teaching, then back on the bus to the Northridge campus for evening classes and workshops. The routine was grueling but fell far short of preparing Rhee for what awaited her in Baltimore. "Back in those days—I was the third TFA class—they hadn't yet figured out how best to train us."

At Northridge, Teach for America assigned dorm rooms in alphabetical order of last names and that's how the school assignments were made. So off to Baltimore went the late-alphabet buddies she had roomed with: Liz Peterson, Deepa Purohit, Rhee, and Rosemary Ricci, who would become her Baltimore roommates and longtime friends.

One by one, the other TFA teachers got snapped up by Baltimore schools. But not Rhee. Even two days before classes started, Rhee had no school that wanted her. "I never got called into interviews. It was a little disconcerting. I think part of it was probably that people were hesitant to hire a Korean person in an African American community. They thought this was not going to be the best match. The white girls didn't seem to have any problems finding jobs." What Rhee opts not to point out is that being Korean may have held particular weight in inner-city Baltimore, where Koreans ran the tiny corner stores and relations with African Americans were fractious, as the store owners often accused their customers of being threatening, thieves, or both. It was not promising chemistry.

Despite not having an assignment, Rhee was told to report to Harlem Park Elementary—just in case. "I show up at the school, walk in the office, and they say, 'Who are you?'" She was shunted off to the faculty room to wait. Eventually, the principal came in to say she had two openings, one in second grade, the other in fifth grade. 'Which do you want?' Replied a startled Rhee, "Does this mean I have a job?" Rhee chose second grade, the grade level she had observed in Los Angeles.

"Hey, (Insert Last Name) Shut Up!"

The first day of school—Rhee's first day as a professional—went reasonably well. She wore a "businessy" outfit supplied by her mother and stood on the playground with a sign to collect her students: Room 213. In fact, the first couple of weeks went well. "They had assigned me a paraprofessional, an older African American woman who scared the crap out of the kids. She kept everyone in line, so much so I actually wanted her to loosen up. Any time a kid would do anything, she'd say, 'Hey, shut up!' The kids were not messing around." Rhee quickly mastered the school jingle: "Harlem Park is the place to be . . . . The place to be is Harlem Park. I am here to learn and so are you, so let's all do our part!" Things were looking good.

All that changed, however, when then-Baltimore Mayor Kurt Schmoke hired a Minnesota-based company to take over failing schools. Harlem Park was among the worst in the city and the school turnaround company concluded that aides should have bachelor's degrees. Out went the tough-ass, undereducated black assistant. "Instead, they gave me this crazy seventy-year-old white guy, Mr. Novak. The kids called him 'Mr. No Shoes.'" According to Rhee, he was even more clueless than she was. Once the assistant disappeared, so did any semblance of classroom control. "My classroom turned into a complete and utter nightmare. It was crazy. This was not just kids acting up. This was literally out of control. One day I walked in and saw the kids standing in a line. I had been trying to get them to stand in line for six weeks. I thought, good, they finally learned. But when I got closer, I realized they were standing in line because they were taking turns running across the room, jumping across a chair and doing flips onto the bean bag. This was not a matter of kids making smart-alecky remarks during a lesson. There was screaming, punching. At one point one kid had another in a headlock and I could see the kid's eyes bulging and red. Literally, the kid was about to be strangled. I had to use every bit of my strength to wedge my hip in between and pry them apart. If I hadn't done that the kid would have passed out. When I tell these stories I always get asked: 'How bad can eight-year-olds be?' But children in my class were getting hurt on a daily basis."

After seeing one of her biggest troublemakers turn meek after entering another teacher's classroom, Rhee's doubts about her abilities deepened. How could the little girl who was a terror in her classroom instantly become a model student, hands folded, paying attention, and raising her hand to answer questions? "I thought, 'Oh, my gosh, it's me, it's not the kids.'" Things got even more depressing when outside evaluators from the University of Maryland, Baltimore, arrived to observe classes. "These mentor ladies pulled me aside and said, 'We believe your classroom is a dangerous place for children and we think you should reconsider this as a career.' I was thinking, 'Thanks for your vote of confidence.'" But Rhee knew they were right. Was she being selfish simply by trying to persevere? "Should I quit not because I can't hack it but because these children are worse off with me than someone else? I had a ton of difficulty trying to reconcile all that in my head."

Although Rhee doesn't mention it now, her roommates recall the epithets she faced. "There were these crazy racist remarks flung at her: 'You're Chinese, you're a chink,'" according to one roommate. The most humiliating comment, however, had nothing to do with race. One day a school librarian briefly took over Rhee's class. Returning to the room, Rhee found the students quietly listening to the librarian. As soon as the librarian left, the students fell into chaos. Rhee pulled one boy aside later and asked why they behaved for the librarian and not for her. He told her: "Because she knows what she's doing."

Not one of the roommates was having an easy time in her school but everyone agreed that Rhee, assigned to the most dangerous neighborhood and serving as the sole TFAer in that school, had it roughest. Liz Peterson arranged for her children at a nearby elementary school to be pen pals with Rhee's students. Even though their schools were only four blocks apart, these children led such narrow lives that those four blocks were a world away; they might as well have been writing to schoolchildren in Hong Kong. When Peterson proposed bringing her students to a field day with Rhee's students, the kids were wary—they had heard Harlem Park was even tougher than their own neighborhood.

Rhee and her roommates lived in a townhouse in Upper Fells Point. At night they worked off their stress by sitting in front of the TV, watching *Roseanne* reruns, grading papers, and eating Taco Bell burritos. Rhee, a junk food junkie, went through rivers of Coke and mounds of bean burritos that year. Together they would pray for snow days. Occasionally, when the days got really rough, they played a money-in-the-bank game: "How much money would you pay to not have to go to school tomorrow?" Actually, the humor was designed to keep them from giving up, no matter how bad it got. "Some corps members were quitting or not coming back a second year," Peterson said. "That was not an option in our house, not something to even consider, because once quitting was on the table it would be hard to say no." Still, the allure of quitting was always there. For these three, all graduates of elite colleges, that turbulent year of teaching was their first flirtation with failure. "We had always been successful at everything we had done," said Ricci, now Rosemary Ricci Mullen. "This was the first time we were flailing or not doing as well as we thought we should. We had obstacles we didn't know how to deal with."

They all worked hard to succeed but the roommates agree that nobody worked harder than Rhee. "I'd go over to their house at night to watch TV and do work," said Roger Schulman, another Baltimore TFAer, "and I remember finding Rhee on the floor with all this stuff laid out. She was going to teach fractions the next day and she was going to use pizzas to do it. Most of us, if we were going to do that, would take a piece of construction paper, draw a circle and draw in some pepperonis. But I watched Michelle cut out a tan piece for the crust, then a red piece for the sauce, yellow for the cheeses—and then she hand-cut pepperonis. And she was doing this for each student."

After the first year was over, the roommates all agreed they needed a break and took off for a cross-country trip to the West Coast. Except Rhee. "Michelle stayed back, working nonstop over the summer, preparing for the next year. I remember her sitting on the floor with a pile of things to do, trying to build a learning center with manipulatives," said Ricci, referring to hands-on tools for learning, used most often in math. If the children weren't behaving and weren't learning—if they were being disrespectful—Rhee blamed herself. "Michelle kept a comment jar on her desk," said Schulman, "and kids could put in any kind of comment they wanted." Including comments on how much they disliked the teacher. One little girl wrote, "On me nerves you get Ms. Rhee." Michelle's reaction: "See, I'm not teaching them enough. Look at how they write!"

The fear of failure was there but more terrifying to Rhee was the fear of never becoming a successful teacher. "I became obsessed with my kids. I would get to school early and a lot of students would come early. I would leave late and a lot would stay late. On weekends I would be picking kids up and taking them places." It was during that first year when Rhee decided to reward a few students with an outing to Baltimore's Inner Harbor. Everything went well until that evening when she tried to drop them off at their homes and discovered that one little girl, who had AIDS, didn't know where she lived. "I started to freak out. The other kids didn't know where she lived. I was like, 'What do you mean you don't know where you live?'" As Rhee's anxiety level grew, she could hear the little girl in the back seat chanting over and over: "Four people in the car, only three know where they live. But there are four people in the car." When Rhee tells the story today, she laughs about both the chant and her naiveté. She had remembered to get permission slips from the parents but never asked for home addresses in advance. That night, however, there was nothing funny about the dilemma. After dropping off the other three children she took the little girl by the hand and began walking through the neighborhoods asking people on the streets if they knew her. Eventually, someone recognized her. "After that I always got everyone's addresses."

That Christmas, she returned to Toledo. It wasn't a pretty sight. "I had (stress) welts all over my body and my mother said, 'See, this is a crazy idea. Stay home. You don't have to go back. You can apply for law school.'" Usually, it was Inza applying the pressure. Not this time. "My father handed me the suitcase and said, 'Suck it up. You've never failed at anything. You're not a quitter. You made the decision . . . now go do it.'" Shang recalls the moment. "I told her that what she was doing was very worthwhile. I told her that when I came to the United States I didn't speak much English and was thrown into work as a [medical] intern. It was really stressful. In this society, especially as a minority, we have to go through this."

SUCKING IT UP

Determined to turn things around, she asked the teacher who settled down the unruly child for advice. "I remember her saying, 'Every day you have to do something fun and unexpected. You can't make it boring.'" That prompted a flurry of experimentation. "If one thing didn't work, then two days later I'd try something else. Slowly, things improved, in part because the students realized I wasn't going to leave."

Progress was slow—a bad day followed a good day. Rhee went through a series of teaching interns that year, all of them bailing out on her. Only one, Deonne Medley, stuck it out, despite the rough initiation. "I came at the beginning of April and things were kind of chaotic. The kids were having a field day. They were running around the room. A couple of kids went on rampages, throwing chairs across the room. Some were blatantly rude. If one person acted up, there was a domino effect and everyone started acting up."

At some point late in the school year, Rhee started seeing one good day following another. Some of the improvement came from small adjustments, such as changing the seating arrangements. Simply shifting the students from tables to a U shape facing her produced huge gains. "I pulled out a couple of kids who couldn't be within touching distance of others and put them in the middle of the U." Another simple strategy: writing kids' names on the board when they did something good, then putting stars next to their names when they did good things. "For the kids who were my biggest behavior problem, I had to write their name immediately when they did anything good. It could be as simple as sitting down. I had to have stars up on the board to erase when they were bad." At the end of the day, the stars earned tickets that could be traded in the class "store" for items such as candy and pencils.

The desk rearrangement combined with the star system—added to the bee-eating incident—worked. "I remember the two ladies from the University of Maryland, Baltimore returning at the end of the year. They told me they had never seen a turnaround this significant in their entire careers. They said, 'We literally thought you should have quit.'"

Medley liked working with Rhee so much that she opted to stay with her another year as a teaching assistant rather than taking a teaching assignment of her own. "The kids started coming around," she said. "They could see that Michelle was really interested in their well-being and that she was coming back every day, she wasn't giving up. The next year her classroom became the showroom classroom, the one the principal would bring visitors to see. Michelle became the go-to teacher."

And so Michelle Rhee's first year of teaching ended on a positive note, a long way from the way it started, a time when, in Rhee's own words, "I sucked."

Harlem Park: Years Two and Three

"Between the first and second years, I became a woman obsessed. I was not going to relive the first year, not going to make any of the same mistakes. I was going to be more prepared than anyone could be. I didn't work that summer—it was the first summer since I was thirteen I didn't work. I didn't have a lot of books, so I went to my father's office and spent the whole day photocopying books. I had a bunch of aunts visiting from Korea, so I literally had this little sweatshop of Koreans cutting stuff out. I had gotten training about how to teach math to kids and a lot of it had to do with manipulatives. Every day, we would be there cutting out bags and bags of shapes."

Returning to Harlem Park, Rhee found a new principal, Linda Carter, who was so impressed when listening to Rhee's plans for the upcoming year that she allowed her to form a team of teachers and mentor two newcomers. In Rhee's words, "That was a little crazy." But it clicked. One teacher took language arts and social studies while Rhee took math and science. "We would then switch and have the other person's group.

That was extremely helpful. I could really focus on creating a great lesson plan for two subjects. I learned how to teach math like nobody's business."

Rhee learned a teaching program called "calendar math," which used the calendar as a central theme from which dozens of activities could be developed. "I had this whole routine I would spin through. I would put different shapes on the calendar, such as bundles of straw. If I got ten bundles, I would teach place value. So if it was March 28, the number would be 28. I would have coins that had Velcro on them and I would ask the kids what combination of coins made 28 cents and they would put that up on the Velcro strip. All this was stuff I did the summer before."

THE MOMENT OF TRANSFORMATION

"I started this thing called 'incredible equations' and it got a life of its own. If the date was the 2nd, they would come up with an equation that equals 2. At first they would do easy things like 1 plus 1. Then some of the brighter kids would come up with 100–98. Then I would teach them different things, like a different way to say 100 is 10 squared. These are things you don't teach second-graders, but it got a life of its own. They came up with ridiculous equations, so I would need to teach them about things like parentheses, so they were learning these rules in a natural way. These observers came into my room one day and the kids were doing these equations and I wasn't thinking about it. They were cubing and squaring and subtracting and these people in the back of my classroom started clapping. This was the point where I realized what we were doing was not normal. Then one day

I was doing calendar math and I was called to the door by the assistant principal. So I called this one kid to the front to continue. And it was fascinating because this kid ran calendar math the exact way I did. There was such consistency with the routine. The kids knew. After that day I didn't run calendar math again. A different kid would do it every day."

That breakthrough, one of several Rhee would experience in her three years in Baltimore, is what Teach for America founder Wendy Kopp refers to as transformative. "The experience of teaching successfully in urban and rural areas is completely transformative," said Kopp. "Ultimately it is the foundational experience of great educational leadership. If you're a teacher in a class of kids who are far behind, and you put them on a level playing field you know what the rest of America doesn't know, which is that this is not a function of kids' lack of motivation or the fact that their parents don't care. This is clearly that kids have not gotten the opportunity they deserve, and you realize that this is a solvable problem, this is within our control. And once you realize that, you can never leave it—your sense of responsibility for solving the problem is just massive."

In Rhee's third year at Harlem Park, she teamed up with another teacher, bringing two classes into a single classroom. "We created this entire system in which reading and math were based on centers. There were six centers for each subject area and the kids would rotate through all six centers in two-hour blocks. My biggest problem was that I couldn't teach them how to read. I mastered math the year before, but I just didn't have the equivalent of calendar math to figure out how to teach reading."

In the summer of 1995, before Rhee started her third year at Harlem Park, she had met fellow TFAer Kevin Huffman at a Teach for America Summer Institute in Houston where they were training new corps members. Huffman, a graduate of Swarthmore, was teaching a first- and second-grade bilingual class in Houston. Rhee took up Huffman's offer to visit his classroom in Houston to learn how he taught reading. "So I went to his classroom and realized that he could teach reading but sucked at math. So we swapped. I set up and taught calendar math and he set up the direct reading instruction. So that became my thing. I stole all his stuff and photocopied it—probably against the law. But I had all the kids reading."

With the boost in reading instruction, the shared "center" classroom became a learning factory. In the center structure, kids didn't work off desks but rather out of tubs kept under their chairs. "We had an egg timer with twelve minutes on it. We had very structured routines. When the egg timer would go off and they would get their tubs and move to the next center. I probably spent a few thousand dollars of my own money on classroom supplies but we made it fun."

According to Rhee, all this paid off in startling test score gains. According to the résumé turned over to Washington, D.C.'s City Council at her 2007 nomination hearing, after two years, 90 percent of her students were scoring at the 90th percentile on national reading and math tests. Only two years earlier, when they first started with Rhee, they were scoring on average at the 13th percentile. At the hearing, there was no shortage of skepticism about those gains. Classroom-level data that could prove or disprove those claims are unavailable, Baltimore officials told the press. Both Rhee's principal, Linda

Carter, and Rhee's coteacher recalled sharp gains but lacked hard evidence. "They tested extremely well," Carter told me. "She didn't make it up."[1] The belief that Rhee exaggerated the gains, however, quickly became an article of faith among Rhee's critics. In 2010, three years after those hearings, I met then-Washington Teachers Union Vice President Nathan Saunders at a Capitol Hill Dunkin' Donuts. The first topic he raised, while laughing and rolling his eyes, was Rhee's impossible "miracle" in Baltimore. In late November 2010, Saunders won an election to take over as WTU president.

Regardless of the exact size of the student gains, the success in Baltimore transformed Rhee and shaped everything that would follow in Washington, D.C. When Rhee arrived in Washington, D.C., and spoke at press conferences and her nomination hearing, Kopp could hear the Baltimore experience in most of what Rhee was saying. "Every other word, Michelle was talking about the sense of possibility. These are the core values of TFA. That sense of possibility, the relentless pursuit of results. You could just hear the absolute sense of urgency and absolute focus in her talk." And as Rhee immediately drew criticism for honing in on a single reform—teacher quality—Kopp was not surprised. "I would run into these people saying, 'You know she hasn't put out an instructional plan.' Right, she doesn't think it is about an instructional plan. She thinks it is about talent, leadership, accountability, culture, all the basics." All the basics Rhee learned in Baltimore. Eating the bee not included.

Among those working at Harlem Park, however, test score gains are not how Rhee is remembered. It was that crazy trip to Cleveland. "By the middle of my third year I realized that the kids had no exposure to the outside world.

I remember asking one of the kids what he wanted to do and he said he wanted to be the pizza delivery guy. The only male he knew that was employed and not on drugs was a delivery guy for Pizza Hut and this is what he was reaching out to. So I wanted to expose them to everything I could. We did a big thing on Kwanzaa and I had people ask why I was teaching their kids Jewish things. So I decided I should do Jewish things as well and a rabbi came in.

"My big thing was to try to get them out of Baltimore. So many of them hadn't been out of a ten-block radius. So I did all this research and discovered that Southwest Airlines had a special deal where you could fly from Baltimore to Cleveland for $45, so that became my big thing. I was going to take these kids on a plane ride. We did fund-raisers, 50–50 raffles. I had every Korean doctor in Toledo sponsoring a couple of kids. So we took the entire third-grade class of, like, 140 kids to Cleveland. It was probably a ridiculous sight. The funniest thing was when I told them we were going to Ohio, and that's where I was from, they kept asking me how they were going to talk to people. I wasn't paying attention at first but then I realized that they thought it was going to be Korea and people were only going to speak Korean.

"So we went on this trip and rented twelve vans and stayed in a Days Inn. My parents drove over and helped chaperone. We did normal stuff, like a ferry cruise on Lake Erie, the natural history museum, the zoo, a movie. We ate half our meals at the Old Country Buffet and that was fantastic. Afterward, they talked about that trip like it was the best thing ever."

That third year of teaching in Baltimore was also the time when the romance between Rhee and Huffman got serious.

Their first meeting in Houston at the TFA Summer Institute was all business. "I remember thinking he was funny and smart but not my type." Huffman's first impression of Rhee was equally ambivalent. "My first memory of her was sitting in a group-training meeting. At the end of the day they had some sort of Jeopardy game to test whether we had learned what we were supposed to learn. And this smart-ass Korean woman in the back of the room starts answering all the questions and celebrating while she's answering them." Huffman, sitting in a Washington, D.C., coffee shop as we talk, starts laughing and pumping his fist in the air and chanting "whoo hoo" to imitate what Rhee was like that day. "I remember thinking, who is this person and why does she think she should answer all the questions like that? So, that was my first impression."

Soon, however, Rhee's assertiveness acquired a certain charm. Early in the summer session all the TFA trainees were assigned to go out into the neighborhoods and recruit students for the summer program run by the institute. Needless to say, enticing low-income black and Latino kids into a nonmandatory summer classes was a daunting task. The TFA trainees split up into groups and headed off to different parts of the city. To give everyone an incentive, the recruitment effort became a contest: who could sign up the most kids? Huffman and Rhee ended up in the same car headed to one of Houston's housing projects. "We had more optimism than sense," said Huffman. "We drove to the projects because that's where the kids were. Most of us went around very tepidly knocking on doors. Not Michelle. She was grabbing kids as they wandered by and saying, 'Little boy, can you take me to your mother right now? I need to talk to her.' Most of the youths were so shocked they did exactly what Rhee asked them to do. At the end of the day, when all the groups reported their results, most had signed up eight or nine students. "Our group signed up like fifty-seven students," said Huffman, due almost entirely to Rhee's fearlessness. "It was hilarious . . . and emblematic of my experiences with Michelle."

Later, when Huffman visited Rhee's Harlem Park school he got an insight into her fearlessness. Although both Huffman and Rhee taught low-income, minority children, there was no comparison. On parent's night at Huffman's Latino school, for example, nearly all the children had an adult show up on their behalf. It might have been an older sibling or cousin but someone showed up. On parent's night at Harlem Park, by contrast, Rhee was lucky to see a handful of parents. And the difference in school culture was startling. "The first time I visited Harlem Park I had a splitting headache by noon because of the noise and chaos in the hallways and around the school," said Huffman. No wonder Rhee was fearless in the Houston projects, he realized. In comparison with the Harlem Park neighborhoods, the Houston projects were practically the suburbs.

As the two began to date, Rhee visited Huffman's classroom in Houston where Huffman had initially been discouraged by the poor reading abilities he found among his students. His school used direct instruction reading— a highly scripted form of instruction that emphasized phonics. Huffman makes no apologies for embracing direct instruction, which is detested by many teachers for its formulaic style. Most teachers prefer a broader curriculum. "I didn't want to hear about the broad-based curriculum. Kids there couldn't read. Children need to be able to read and they need to be able to do some basic math. That was my mind-set."

Huffman's biggest challenge was his lack of direct instruction materials written in Spanish. So he wrote his own materials. "My students just started killing it in reading, both in terms of their ability to read words and also comprehend." On one visit to Houston Rhee accompanied Huffman as an extra chaperone on a school outing to NASA. On the bus, students from another teacher's class started singing all the songs they had learned in that class. After several songs, a student from Huffman's class loudly asked: "How come we don't know any of these songs?" Rhee's response: "Because your teacher was busy teaching you how to read!"

Through the multiple visits, the dating turned serious. "He won me over," said Rhee. "He's a funny guy and very endearing." During the school year they dated, Huffman watched Rhee's politics shift. "Michelle was a flaming liberal coming out of college. At one point she was considering going into labor relations, and not on the side that people might think." During her initial Teach for America training friends recall her walking around with a backpack that had one pro-choice button and one anti-Bush button. "She went off to her [Baltimore] school fairly naively, as a lot of us in TFA did, just pro-union, pro-labor," said Huffman. And then reality intervened.

Part of the friction with other teachers arose when Harlem Park was turned over to Minneapolis-based Education Alternatives Inc. to experiment with a new teaching model.[2] The "whole child" approach known as Tesseract was not embraced by most of the teachers at Harlem Park. Many had the attitude of here's another case where the white man is coming into our school and telling us what to do. But Rhee made it work in her classroom, which left her puzzled. Considering the track record of failure at Harlem Park, why won't the teachers give this a chance? Said Hoffman, "She came at from an innocent perspective of 'I don't get this.' We're all struggling and failing and they've given us something and it works. Why does everybody have to fight it all the time?" When Rhee chose to embrace the model—even speaking to outside groups about how Tesseract could work—other teachers at Harlem Park turned against her. "Michelle went to one gathering where a teacher union representative stood up and called her a whore," said Huffman.[3] The fact that Rhee was registering such strong academic gains with her students only worsened relations. By her third year at Harlem Park, when Rhee was fund-raising to send the students on the road trip to Cleveland, some of the other teachers declined to help. Another time the vote tally for teacher of the year at Harlem Park was altered during the count in an attempt to keep Rhee from winning, said Huffman.[4]

"A lot of us came into Teach for America naive, in the good sense," said Huffman. "We felt like if we found something that's good for kids, everyone was going to embrace it. Aren't we all in the same struggle together? I think Michelle was honestly shocked to find that some teachers would actually rather fail than concede a political point."

This was an exciting time for both Huffman and Rhee. They were succeeding with their students and diving into school reform issues that were new to them, such as whether teachers should be held accountable for student learning. If they could boost student learning in their classrooms, why was there such indifference among so many other teachers? "We were both data hounds," said Huffman. "We were both aggressively pro-accountability before accountability was something people were talking about. We didn't want to hear complaining and whining about what the barriers were. We were all about just getting the job done." Their early innocence about how urban schools operated wore off quickly.

On one visit to Baltimore Rhee went to pick up Huffman at the airport and discovered he wasn't on the plane. Instead, she found someone holding a sign with her name on it who informed her, "Come with me." She took a waiting limo to a hotel and found Huffman in a room with flowers and a wedding proposal. "It was very cool." After a year's engagement—the time Inza Rhee said it would take to plan a wedding—they got married August 17, 1996, in Toledo at the Museum of Art. Shortly after the wedding Huffman left for law school at New York University and Rhee left for Harvard's Kennedy School. Soon, they would both return to education with two deep imprints from Houston and Baltimore: inner city students can achieve but considerable obstacles stand in the way—obstacles that need removing.

Chapter Three

GOING NATIONAL

In her book, *One Day, All Children. . . ,*[1] Wendy Kopp describes the launch of an ambitious new Teach for America offshoot called TEACH! Its goal was to spark "systemic" reform by propelling TFA from a niche provider of promising teachers from elite colleges to a broad-based supplier of high-quality teachers to school districts. During Kopp's never-ending campaign to raise money for TFA, that's what funders always said they wanted—systemic reform. "At first I wasn't completely clear what 'systemic' meant," writes Kopp, "but ultimately I gathered it referred to programs that would effect fundamental, far-reaching, long-term change."

On paper, TEACH! did just that by setting up local organizations that recruited, selected, and trained teachers for districts that would pay TFA for that service. Again, on paper, TEACH! appeared to solve two problems for the cash-strapped TFA: provide a steady income source and spark new foundation funding, all while continuing the national service of funneling more high-quality teachers into school districts.

It didn't work out that way. In Kopp's book, the creation of TEACH! falls in the chapter called "The Dark Years."

What looked like a great idea—and it was a great idea—confused funders. "They didn't understand the relationship between Teach for America and TEACH!" writes Kopp. "They thought we were taking on too much. Neither did they see why we needed a whole organization to help districts recruit and train teachers; wouldn't it be easier simply to lobby for the changes to take place? And how could we hope to revolutionize teacher quality without working with schools of education? After all, it was schools of education that provided the vast majority of the nation's teachers."

Kopp thought the funders were missing the point. In hindsight she was right. But the funders were right as well about the new enterprise being too much for TFA. The program divided the staff into two groups that undermined each other. Plus, the new appendage sapped precious financing. In 1995 Kopp shut down TEACH! to focus on TFA but planned for an eventual rebirth. In 1997 that opportunity arose and for its first employee Kopp reached out to someone she barely knew: Michelle Rhee.

TAKING ON A NEW (TEACHER) PROJECT

Kopp first heard about Rhee from her work as a trainer with TFA's Summer Institute. "I just heard she was incredibly effective," said Kopp in an interview at TFA's New York City headquarters. Kopp laughed as she related one thing she knew about Rhee at the time: "I heard she was very stylish, looking like a million bucks as she went off every morning to visit her corps members."

Kopp found Rhee at Harvard's Kennedy School, where she was earning her master's degree in public policy. Rhee was interested but also hesitant. The Rhee who would take D.C. by storm was still a ways off. Within two years, however, Kopp would turn over the entire organization—now renamed The New Teacher Project (TNTP)—to Rhee, who worried over whether she was up to the challenge, especially her ability to deal with the board of directors at the new organization. "She wasn't hyperconfident but I told her I would explain the board thing. It was so clear she could do it," said Kopp.

As TNTP's president, Rhee made some early decisions that proved to have long-term implications, all for the good. Because she disliked private fund-raising, she decided to make TNTP a revenue-generating operation. "I'd rather hustle for a contract any day than have to ask somebody to give me money. We would measure our success based on whether or not the services we were providing were valuable enough that school districts would pay for them. If they weren't willing to pay for them, then what we were offering wasn't having any value."

Although in later years TNTP would shift to a different financing model, eschewing grant money in the beginning proved invaluable. "We could work with the clients we wanted to work with . . . because we didn't have funders saying, 'Oh, we want to you to go to this city or that city.' I think that's a problem in education philanthropy today because so many things are driven by the funders and in a really perverse, not good way." Rhee's hesitations about aligning her work with foundations' goals would carry over into her D.C. tenure because foundations rushed in to help what they saw as a bold reformer only to receive what they, at times, perceived to be a cold shoulder—at least compared to the usual warm reception they were accustomed to getting.

The second decision Rhee made early on was that the group would not develop a national identity akin to the brand name nurtured by Teach for America. When TNTP entered into contracts with school districts to recruit high-quality, often nontraditional teachers, such as career-changers, the program would always get named after the school district— Teach Baton Rouge, the New York City Teaching Fellows, Massachusetts Bonus Program—rather than be called The New Teacher Project. "I avoided becoming a lightning rod like Wendy and TFA were at the time."[2] Plus, that brought TNTP good will with the school districts that hired them. For a lot of those superintendents, the best press they got was press through TNTP's teacher recruitment program—and the districts got full credit for it.

· · · · ·

Rhee built a unique team at TNTP, some of whom would come with her to run DCPS. One pick was a friend from the Kennedy School, Layla Avila, who had arrived late to the Kennedy program because of a summer job. By that time, the students had already divided up into all-important, and often cliquey, study groups.

Avila asked a friend about joining his study group, to which Rhee belonged, and the friend began bargaining with the other group members. Avila recalled, "Some of them were like, 'Well, I don't know, we're already kind of big, we don't know.' They were making a big deal of it and I was standing there while they were having this conversation. Then, out of nowhere, Michelle says, 'Well, if this study group is too big and you guys won't let her join, I can just break off and Layla and I can start our own study group.' What was so interesting is she didn't even know me. We had not even introduced ourselves." But the study group members knew how smart and organized Rhee was. And they knew that she was a leader in the conversations about case studies. The idea of Rhee leaving was scary. "So when she said that, they all panicked and were like, 'No, no, no, no. . . . We can make room for Layla.' . . . It shows Michelle is not going to put up with that nonsense about being selective and exclusive."

Influenced by Rhee's enthusiasm for TFA, Avila joined the corps after earning her degree from the Kennedy School, spending two years in the Compton Unified School District outside Los Angeles. When her two years at TFA were up, Rhee approached her about coming aboard to run The New Teacher Project contract with the Compton schools.

Another pick for The New Teacher Project was Tim Daly, who as an undergraduate at Northwestern University entered an American Studies program that examined the big social issues ranging from health care to the future of capitalism. "People had very different ideas about how American political life should be organized and what welfare for adults should be like," Daly said. "But almost everyone agreed that none of the systems would work if we did not provide a really good educational base for kids."

That consensus probably explains why a third of the students in that American Studies program entered Teach for America. Daly was assigned to a middle school in Baltimore, arriving in summer 1999, hired sight unseen by a principal who regularly reached out to TFA. The principal's assistant, who had seen a lot of idealistic young teachers arrive—and depart quickly—looked Daly up and down. "I remember him saying something like, 'Well, welcome, for as long as it lasts.'"

What looked like a potential horror show—as many as forty students assigned to a class held in an open classroom with no walls separating the adjoining class (a generally disastrous education fad of the 1970s)—turned into a transformative experience for Daly. "I looked forward to every single day. I had such a ball teaching," he said. He was especially inspired by one of his TFA roommates who taught introductory science for a class of students with limited math skills. The class had an official enrollment of more than seventy students because the school correctly assumed that only a fraction of those students would actually show up. The roommate decided to scuttle the curriculum and instead teach physics. "His goal was to get the kids to pass the Maryland state physics test and many did. He got them to go against the norms of a school where the least cool thing you could possibly do was to get engaged in a math or science class."

That was just one example of the inspiration Daly saw in some teachers. "Nothing stopped these teachers," he said. "They would come to work every day well-planned, totally focused, and they did not accept the idea that because our kids had very difficult home lives that they couldn't do great stuff while they were in school. . . . I think people consistently underestimate the resiliency and the fire kids have. It was just so patently obvious that we could do a much better job—because these teachers were doing it." That was Daly's transformation. Just as Kopp predicts: once you see it being done, you can't just walk away. So after hearing Michelle Rhee at a conference talking about The New Teacher Project, he applied.

· · · · ·

One unusual hire for Rhee was on the business side. Ariela Rozman came not from teaching but from the for-profit world. When Rhee found her, Rozman had worked as a consultant for Bain & Company ("Bain is an excellent company but I realized I was working really hard to make rich people richer.") and then for an online pharmacy. "I had no education background other than education had always been my passion," she said. She had heard of TNTP, applied, and had a phone interview with Rhee, who after fifteen minutes on the phone offered Rozman the job on the spot and wanted to know if she would accept. Surprised by Rhee's decisiveness, she had to backtrack to talk about issues such as salary. "I don't want to be greedy but are there any details around this?"

Rozman's first meeting with Rhee included a group of refined White House staffers at Washington's stately Hay-Adams Hotel. "Everyone had a salad or a little light lunch," Rozman recalled. "When we were asked about dessert, everyone said 'no, no, no,' all the way around, until the waiter got to Michelle, who said she was going to have the crème brûlée. And she proceeded to eat it, savoring every bite while everyone sat around. I thought: this is going to be a good boss to work for."[3]

Rozman's first assignment was to talk to all the "partners"—the TNTP employees who sold teacher recruitment contracts to school districts—and devise a new marketing strategy. "One of the things I heard constantly from every single person I interviewed was that you just need to follow Michelle around and write down everything she does and then figure out how to teach the rest of us to do that. So I would. I would follow her around and try to write down everything she said but I cautiously had to ask, 'Can you speak slower?' It didn't take me long to figure out that wasn't going to work."

After Rozman was in the job a month, the federal government offered a grant supporting career-changers going into teaching. Before then, TNTP had not sought government grants but Rhee decided this was a perfect fit. She assigned Rozman to handle the grant writing. "I said, 'There is no way I can do this,'" Rozman recalled. "'I don't know the organization and I'm not a grant writer.' But Rhee said, 'I know you can do this. We will support you and I know you will do an excellent job.' That kind of confidence from Michelle was consistent. She does a fantastic job of just being able to see where the bar is set. The end of the story is that we got the grant for $2 million. About two days after the notice I get a FedEx package and inside is this lovely Kate Spade briefcase with a note from Michelle saying, 'Thank you so much for your excellent work.' I get paid a salary to do this; I have never had someone give me a gift for doing what I thought was my job."

That became Rhee's style. Although she ran the organization largely from a distance—living in different cities and managing by e-mail—she kept things personal. Recalled Daly: "She was very good about recognizing staff and there was never a one-size-fits-all gift. For instance, if she found out someone was working insane hours, she would call them and let them know that she bought them a spa gift certificate and was mailing it. It wasn't like you were getting a paperweight with your name on it."

Another insight into Michelle's management style emerged when TNTP decided to move site manager Candice Frazier from Louisiana to Memphis. "Usually," Frazier says, "I would move myself but given the short time frame—I needed to be in Memphis in two to three weeks—The New

Teacher Project agreed to pay for a moving company." Frazier found a company, which cited Better Business Bureau credentials, and arranged for the move. On the day her belongings were supposed to arrive in Memphis, nobody showed. The company gave a succession of new arrival times but after about two weeks Frazier realized the drivers had absconded with her life belongings. "I had arrived in Memphis with my dog and one suitcase with clothes," she said. "I was sleeping on the floor with a comforter and eating off one plate with one fork and one knife."

When Rhee found out, she mobilized the company, coming up with the funds to help Frazier rebuild her life. "She moved for this organization," Daly said, "and even though money is tight there is no way she is going to eat this herself. Michelle was more adamant and more determined than anyone that we had to step up and do this." In the end, Frazier said she received between $6,000 and $7,000 from TNTP to replace her losses. "It showed me that TNTP cared, that we're family," said Frazier. "Michelle went completely above and beyond." Months later, when some of her belongings were found in a storage locker in Texas, Frazier offered to return some of the money but Rhee declined. "She told me I went through a hard time; the money was mine."

· · · · ·

Rhee experienced some scary personal moments of her own during The New Teacher Project years. Her husband finished law school and took a job with a law firm in Washington, D.C., so the family moved there. In December 1998, their first daughter, Starr, was born at Georgetown Hospital. When Starr was one-and-a-half, the family moved to Toledo to be near her parents. They bought a house in nearby Sylvania, a short drive from her family home in Rossford. "The New Teacher Project was really taking off and I was traveling a ton. We needed more help." That's also when Kopp persuaded Huffman to give up his law practice to work for Teach for America. Both did their jobs remotely from Toledo, which was a challenge in those days, when Internet access was more limited. But they needed the help of the Rhee's parents, especially when she became pregnant with Olivia, who was born in March 2002.

Not long after that, Rhee had planned to drop off the girls at her parents' house the night before an early morning trip. "Then my mom called and said she wasn't feeling good and didn't want the girls to get sick. I said fine, we'll drop them off in the morning." In the middle of the night, Inza and Shang awakened to the sound of breaking glass. A fire, apparently caused by an electrical malfunction in the garage, had broken out. Inza and Shang were trapped in their bedroom; they escaped only by tying blankets together and lowering themselves from the bedroom window. "The next day we went to the house and you could see the room where the girls slept. The crib was charred. It was terrifying," Rhee says. The hallway between her parents' bedroom and the girls' room was the escape route blocked by the fire.

The house was a total loss. After the fire, Shang Rhee decided to retire. He had always wanted to retire in Denver, so he was not interested in rebuilding their family home. He only wanted a cash settlement from the insurance company. That job was turned over to Michelle. "I went through a year and an insane amount of time working out their insurance." Still, the company refused to pay. Then, Michelle got invited by Laura Bush, an admirer of her work with The New Teacher Project, as her guest to a State of the Union Address. Toledo's *The Blade* wrote an article about Rhee's appearance on Capitol Hill. "The local insurance guy faxes a copy of the article to the headquarters and says, 'This is the lady you're messing with.'" The next day the insurance company decided to pay. In 2004 the Rhee parents moved to Denver and Michelle and Kevin followed for the same reason they moved to Toledo. They could do their jobs remotely and on-the-run. What they needed the most were Inza and Shang's babysitting services.

One-Two Punch

The big breakthrough for TNTP, for Rhee and the organization, came in two phases. The first arrived with Compton, where the staff, working until 1 a.m., came up with this slogan to attract teachers: "Compton kids deserve a Beverly Hills education." Says Rhee: "It was genius. It was so the right thing." And it worked, triggering a surge in teacher applications.

A few days later the same group came together to discuss how to market the New York City Teaching Fellows Program. They decided on a picture of a little Latino girl and this plea: "Four of five fourth-graders in the city's most challenged schools can't read or write to standards. Are you willing to do something about it?" District officials nixed it, saying it made them look bad. Rhee said she told them, "First of all, it's not that you look bad, you *are* bad! We didn't make up this statistic.' . . . And the second thing is, if you were trying to recruit great people to come into the public school district from another profession, your message can't be: 'Come be a cog in the wheel.' You have to compel them. You have to convince them you can change people's lives and that the situation is really dire."

Then-Chancellor Harold Levy intervened and approved the ad. "We got an unbelievable response," Rhee said. "It was so crazy. The ad ran in *The New York Times*. *The Times* found it such a different ad that they wrote an article about it. Once that happened, it was all over. It was unbelievable. We knew within days that we were going to be able to hit our recruitment numbers."

· · · · ·

Once TNTP gained momentum, Rhee steered it in a very different direction, one that would land her in D.C. as chancellor but also put her on a collision course with Randi Weingarten, the future president of the American Federation of Teachers (AFT). "I had been running The New Teacher Project for several years and I was getting frustrated," Rhee said. She had thought districts might not be finding enough good teaching candidates but that wasn't it. The problem was that none of them were getting hired. "We thought this was crazy," she said. "They were talking about needing more math and science teachers and we'd bring in this astrophysicist who would not get hired."

Rhee decided to investigate the problem—mostly on TNTP's own dime. In 2003 Rhee's investigative team eventually turned out "Missed Opportunities," a journalistic-style probe concluding that the shortage of urban teachers was a myth, even in the supposedly higher-need areas such as math and science.

Hiring rules were part of the problem: teachers didn't have to inform the district they were leaving until the day before school started, and union rules, laid out in contracts, said that no new teachers could be hired until all existing teachers had jobs. If a school was closed or reconstituted,[4] those teachers as well as teachers pushed out by principals unhappy with their performance got first dibs on other positions in the system. By contract, all those teachers were due new jobs. By having to wait until the last minute to find places for unassigned teachers, districts lost their opportunities to hire talented applicants from outside the system. Instead, those teachers had their pick of suburban school districts eager to snap them up. The report not only laid out the problem, with real data, but also suggested solutions. TNTP printed a few hundred copies but that turned out to be not nearly enough. "People on Capitol Hill were reading it, the U.S. Department of Education," Rhee said. "It got huge traction because everyone had a story about it; they all seemed to know of some young teacher who wanted to teach in an urban district but never got a call back from HR."

"Missed Opportunities" led to a spurt in investigative reporting on teachers' union contracts—"the most intractable problem," Rhee said. The report compiled data from several districts around the country to show, in Rhee's words, that "it was the lowest-performing kids in the worst schools that were getting screwed the most by these union provisions." Teacher turnover is highest in the lowest-scoring schools, so they are disproportionately harmed by recruitment limitations. The report showed that you can get great teachers in April, but if you have to wait for August, because of contract rules, only the worst candidates are left. "That's really detrimental to the low-performing schools that have ten, twenty, thirty vacancies," she said.

· · · · ·

The "Missed Opportunities" report was followed up by the more specific, more damning, "Unintended Consequences" report of 2005, which laid out the details behind why urban principals are unable to select their own teachers. Both reports caught the attention of then-New York City Public Schools Chancellor Joel Klein. "When I got here, the human resource people were skeptical about The New Teacher Project because they didn't come with the seal of approval with the United Federation of Teachers (UFT)," said Klein. The UFT is the New York arm of the American Federation of Teachers and was led at the time by Randi Weingarten. "At that point our HR department was sort of integrated almost with the UFT, and I mean that seriously," said Klein. Klein launched a shake-up, part of which included expanding the New York City Teaching Fellows program, run by TNTP.

Naturally, Klein wanted to meet Rhee. But she wasn't what he expected. "When I first met her, she seemed sur-prisingly kind of quiet and cautious," he said. "I would not have predicted, based on that first meeting, that Michelle Rhee would turn out to be the bomb-thrower that we have now witnessed on the cover of *Time*, broom in hand. But she was obviously thoughtful, and from the first time I met her through today, we have a mind lock about how to think about the problems, how to navigate the political issues that surround them. And there are not a ton of people like that I've encountered in my eight years I've been doing this work."

Klein was convinced not only that teacher effectiveness was the paramount school reform, but also that it could be measured. That was, and is, a radical proposition. Usually, teachers are never measured for their effectiveness. Their pay increases are based on time spent in the classroom and extra academic credentials. Klein believed that if he could assess how much each teacher was helping—or hurting—students, he could break through the barriers that caused schools to fail. "The whole education system is built on three pillars of mediocrity: lockstep pay, life tenure, and seniority," he said. "Until we build it on a foundation of performance, accountability, and excellence, we won't succeed."

That's the mind lock he shared with Rhee. "She understood that a system built on those three pillars isn't going to go away just because Joel Klein says it's not a good idea," Klein said. "She understood the need for disruptive strategies. And disruptive strategies aren't ever going to be just gleefully, cheerfully adopted. Machiavelli figured that out a long time ago. The defenders of the status quo are going to be vehement in their defense, whereas those who stand to benefit from disrupting the status quo"—in this case, students and parents—"don't know who they are and why it matters to them. So the deck is stacked. Michelle understood all these things."

· · · · ·

In New York the ideal disruptive strategy that emerged— embraced by Klein and abetted by Rhee—would launch the latter into a struggle with Randi Weingarten and the AFT. In 2005, Klein's long fight to change UFT work rules fecklessly bartered away by previous New York schools chancellors— rules such as forced hiring of incompetent teachers—finally triggered a hearing. In New York State, unfruitful negotiations with public unions end up before a nonbinding arbitration panel. Although technically nonbinding, both sides acknowledge that the trial before a panel of three arbiters will be the final word on the issue.

Usually, arbitration hearings were about wages but this one was about work rules. Dan Weisberg, who at the time handled Klein's labor negotiations but later joined The New Teacher Project, explained that the goal was to reform "a system where literally thousands of teachers, against their will and against the will of the principals impacted, were forced into positions at schools, sometimes bumping out first-year teachers."

Everything Klein wanted to do was at stake in this one arbitration hearing. If principals couldn't select their own teams, how could he possibly hold them accountable for student achievement? The odds favored the union. Not only was the district not putting up much in the way of salary increases as a bargaining chip, but Weisberg could not find anyone who wanted to testify against the union, which wielded considerable power come election time. "Everyone in the education policy community knew at the time that this was a major fight, a titanic battle between the mayor and Joel Klein on one hand and Randi Weingarten on the other," Weisberg said. "A lot of people wanted no part of it. I mean, there were people I called who were not interested in getting within two hundred miles of it. Up until that time, even when people knew the union contracts were wack, nobody was actually willing to say this is crazy. I told them, 'I think we should say it. I think we should tell everybody that.'"

Weisberg had one person in mind to deliver the message: Michelle Rhee. Not only did Rhee agree to testify but she insisted on a strategy of brutal truth-telling. "I told them we should tell everyone that the union contract was crazy, that it's good for adults and bad for kids," Rhee said.

. . . . .

The confrontation took place at a large law firm in midtown Manhattan, where four long tables were arranged in a square. At the top of the square was the three-person arbitration panel. On one side was the UFT; on the other side, the New York City Department of Education. Anyone testifying sat on the fourth side.

"So you've got Randi Weingarten sitting at one table with an army of lawyers and consultants and union officials," said Weisberg. "I remember going to the UFT holiday party and seeing all these people who were going to run in the Democratic primary for mayor and they were literally striking the most obsequious poses imaginable around her. I mean, they were almost on bended knee. She is a very powerful figure." The small contingent from the Education Department appeared outgunned.[5]

But Rhee had something no one else had: actual data from the two investigations. She was able to lay out, by the numbers, how real children were being hurt, especially children in high-poverty neighborhoods. "Michelle delivered some very powerful, very persuasive testimony that was rooted in data," Weisberg said. "She was able to tell the arbitrators with precision how many teachers are forced placed, where they were forced placed, and what the impact was. And she was able to do it in a way that seemed objective and dispassionate."

Rhee remembers the glare she got from Randi Weingarten: "If looks could kill, I'd be dead. And as I went through my testimony, she was livid. I remember she said a couple of nasty things that day and one was, 'Don't you have a contract with the New York City Department of Education?' Basically, she was saying, 'You made this data up because you want to be in the good graces of Joel Klein.' That was my first taste of how she operates."

In the end, the panel sided almost entirely with Rhee, coming out in favor of getting rid of forced placement in favor of mutual consent, which means a school principal had to agree to take a teacher from another school. No more forced placements. "There's no question about it: this would not have happened if Michelle hadn't had the courage to get involved in this fight," Weisberg said.

"She was dazzling," said Klein. That was the day everything changed. Not only did Klein win a big chunk of what he wanted but now he also had a name of a future star to tuck away in case another mayor called to ask, who can turn around my schools? A scant two years after the arbitration hearing, that opportunity arose in D.C.

· · · · ·

As with most power struggles, tactical victories can complicate strategic ones. When Rhee was hired in D.C., AFT officials with long memories were eager to exact revenge. Abigail Smith, who helped recruit Rhee for Mayor Fenty and later became her "transformation management" chief, recalled an early meeting with union officials after Rhee's appointment was announced. The meeting included Washington Teachers Union President George Parker and at least one AFT official who had been in New York when Rhee testified. Everyone in the meeting was comparing notes on the reaction to Rhee's appointment when the AFT official gleefully announced one comment from a union listserv: "Let's kill the bitch." Smith was astonished this was repeated in a meeting and, she said, so was Parker—though he only told her that afterward.

When Rhee departed The New Teacher Project, she had built a staff of 140 people, an annual budget of $20 million and a reputation among journalists as a go-to group for the inside baseball on teacher quality, a topic that had risen quickly to the top of the education reform agenda. Rhee crafted an organization destined to continue its growth: three years later TNTP had a staff of 210 and an annual budget of $32 million. Looking back, those were the easy years.

Less successful from that period was her marriage. Rhee and Huffman decline to discuss the details but when Rhee landed the job as D.C. schools chancellor they got divorced. "They were very nice and cleared the (D.C.) courtroom," she says, "because they didn't want to make it a spectacle. It was over in 30 minutes."[6]

Chapter Four

WELCOME TO THE NATION'S EDUCATION SUPERFUND SITE

Many great books have been written about big-city corruption. When it comes to the nation's capital, the standout is *Dream City*, by journalists Harry Jaffe and Tom Sherwood[1] The book documents the unraveling of Marion Barry, a charismatic civil rights leader who was elected the first chairman of the Student Nonviolent Coordinating Committee in the 1960s and later rose to become mayor of Washington, D.C., in 1978, bringing with him a "dream team" of black superstars. The book documents Barry's mastery of race politics over his three consecutive terms, his tolerance of corruption, and his ever-escalating appetites for women, booze, and cocaine. To most Americans, Barry will forever be remembered for the events of January 18, 1990, when FBI informant Rasheeda Moore lured him into yet another session with the crack pipe, this time in a thoroughly wired room at D.C.'s Vista International Hotel. Detectives burst through

the door and triggered Barry's famous outburst. From
Dream City:

> "Bitch set me up," he said, interrupting the recitation
> of his rights. He said it again and again like a mantra,
> as if understanding it would make it go away.
>
> "I, I want to call my lawyer right now. I'll be god-
> damn. I got fucked-up here with this goddamn bitch,
> setting me up like this. Set me up, ain't that a bitch."[2]

The book's epilogue documents the fallout from those
corrupt years: the astonishing number of street killings,
the haywire budgets that would later require federal intervention, and the plummeting population, which fell below
six hundred thousand residents in 1993, from a high of eight
hundred thousand in 1950. In the post-Barry years, policing
would improve, the federal District of Columbia Financial
Control Board would reset the District's ledgers, and corporate real estate investors would pour money and new hope
into Washington, D.C.'s economy. If Jaffe and Sherwood
ever updated their book, however, they would have to point
out that one piece of the D.C. scandals never got straightened out: the schools. Under Barry, the schools central office
became an adult employment center, a place to deposit job
seekers. "It was the political machine's way of hiring folks
and securing votes," explains William Wilhoyte, a successful school administrator in the highly respected schools in
neighboring Montgomery County who in 1992 was persuaded by former Montgomery school chief Paul Vance to
come out of retirement and join him as he took over the

reins of D.C. schools. Vance didn't last long but Wilhoyte persisted through several succeeding D.C. superintendents, giving him a unique perspective into how the Barry-inspired, schools-as-employment-centers system worked.[3]

"There was no quality. There was no curriculum. There was no true evaluation. There was no one being held accountable. And there was no good instruction . . . everything you touched in the system felt like a cancer." Wilhoyte visited class after class where there were no real teaching materials. The most common teaching tool used by teachers was five or ten photocopies they'd made of work sheet material, nowhere near enough for an entire class. The teacher would hand them out and then sit behind the desk and wait for the end-of-class bell to ring.

THIRTY-ONE FLAVORS OF FAILURE

All that incompetence, which helped make D.C. schools among the most expensive in the nation, somehow managed to fly under the radar as other parts of the city government got repaired. When Adrian Fenty was elected mayor in 2007, the D.C. schools were thoroughly earning their reputation as the nation's education Superfund site. What's important, however, is *why* they ranked as the worst in the nation. To outsiders, those not working within the system, the reasons involved general incompetence: failing to get schoolbooks delivered, failing to maintain buildings, failing to keep track of who's in the system, and failing to accommodate special education students. All those problems were extensively reported on in *The Washington Post*. What wasn't reported, however, was the attitude *within* the system, which was best summed up in the message of the sign Rhee's team discovered at Slowe Elementary: we're doing the best we can with the flawed children sent our way.

Race and poverty, not ineffective teaching and learning, explained the poor student performance—that was the prevailing attitude among many D.C. educators at the time Rhee arrived. Wilhoyte recalls visiting one school where the students had a 5 percent proficiency rate, meaning 95 percent of the students tested below grade level. "I laid out all the data over the previous five years and asked the administrators, 'What is your acceptable rate of failure?'" Wilhoyte walked them through a series of examples: If you buy a new car, what's your acceptable rate of failure? If you get on an airplane, what's your acceptable rate of failure? And finally, What's your acceptable rate of failure with these children? "They answered they were doing everything they could. And I said, but 95 percent of your students are failing. Who owns this? And they would answer, 'Not us.'" Blaming children and families was pervasive throughout the system, said Wilhoyte. "They would say, 'We're doing our job; it's just them.'"

· · · · ·

Research done for this book concludes just the opposite. It's *not* "just them." Jonathan Mills, a researcher for the Department of Education Reform at the University of Arkansas,[4] compared low-income black students in the District to students from similar backgrounds in New York City, Houston, and Boston. The data reveal sharp differences that can only be explained by school quality. Based on the federal "school report card" known as the National Assessment of Educational Progress (NAEP), D.C. schoolchildren performed substantially worse than their counterparts in the years from

2003 to 2007, the year Michelle Rhee was appointed schools chancellor.

The federal report card includes an important comparison of poor and minority students in nearly a dozen districts around the country called the Trial Urban District Assessment.[5] Across the three testing years examined, the average low-income black child in these school districts was 1.2 years ahead of D.C. students on the fourth-grade math exam, 1.1 years ahead on fourth-grade reading, 1.3 years ahead on eighth-grade math, and 0.8 years ahead on eighth-grade reading.

When compared to children in the higher-performing urban districts of Boston, Houston, and New York City, D.C. students fared especially poorly. "Comparisons of D.C. performance with these districts almost always paint a rather dismal picture of D.C.," says Mills. Low-income black children in both Boston and Houston were 1.8 years ahead of D.C. children during those three years on both the reading and math tests. New York students were 1.9 years ahead of D.C. students in math and 2 years ahead in reading.

Among low-income black eighth-graders, the picture was similarly bleak. During the three years examined, the average child in Boston, Houston, or New York was more than a year ahead of students in D.C. (Boston, 1.5 years ahead; Houston, 1.2 years; and New York, 1.1 years). In math, children in the comparison districts were more than 2 years ahead of D.C. children (Boston, 2 years; Houston, 2.1 years; New York, 1.9 years).

In 2010, New York City Schools Chancellor Joel Klein offered a parallel finding in a commentary that ran in *The Washington Post*.[6] Low-income black fourth- and eighth-grade students in Washington, D.C., Detroit, Milwaukee, and

Los Angeles scored far below similar students in Boston, Charlotte, New York, and Houston. By fourth grade, Klein wrote, "poor African American children in Detroit are already three grades behind their peers in Boston." The difference was not with the students but with the schools, Klein concluded. "Different teachers get very different results with similar students."

The research for this book confirms Klein's observation. When children perform so much worse than others from the same race and family income, you can't blame color or poverty. It has to be the schools. Nothing but bad schools can explain why in 2007 D.C.'s low-income black children scored the worst in the nation on federal reading tests given to fourth-graders. D.C.'s eighth-graders did slightly better: they were only second worst, edged out by students in Los Angeles.

· · · · ·

In Washington, D.C., any schools chief picked by Fenty faced triple hurdles. First, convince a city grown accustomed to viewing the school system as a stable source of employment that schools had to be radically refocused on students. That may sound obvious but in a city such as Washington, D.C., which lacks a manufacturing base, any form of predictable employment—especially a government job—assumes the highest priority. Second, convince parents and voters that weak school leadership and ineffective teaching are the causes of low student achievement. The third goal: restaff schools with effective principals and teachers.

The toughest challenge was transforming expectations about what schools are expected to accomplish. Many in Washington, D.C., simply weren't convinced that bad schools explained the poor student outcomes. Early in my book research

I met with Nathan Saunders, then-vice president of the Washington Teachers Union. Saunders, a former high school government teacher, dismissed the rankings on federal tests that placed the District of Columbia at the bottom of the nation. For starters, D.C. suffers because it's not a state, he explained. "As a result, there's a lack of power we would normally have as a state," he said. "Congress has made us the guinea pigs for everything from school vouchers to charter schools to every choice experiment in the United States. And for what? With the political power we would have as a result of having a House member, a senator, a governor, we would be able to address some of these (education problems) internally."

Then, Saunders shifted to race politics, giving an explanation rarely uttered in public but broadly embraced. Rhee, explained Saunders, doesn't understand black and brown children. "When you say that the most important thing to black and brown children is a teacher, that doesn't work in our community. . . . Historically, our community is family-based and our community is not associated with the concept of a nuclear family. In the black community, if mom and dad weren't cutting the mustard, then there's grandma and uncles and aunts. You understand? And the 'system' has never been the primary source of survival for us. The system has been a place where you were apt to lose your children, where harm could come to the child or to the family unit. And so in our communities we turn inward. You understand? Not to the government programs." Religion and extended family, Saunders said, may play a more important role in the life of a black child than a teacher. "You can't run around and say that the only thing children need is a good teacher." Saunders is no outlier. Former D.C. schools chief Clifford Janey expressed the same sentiment when he asserted that schools are responsible for only a small portion of what children learn.[7]

Saunders has a good point about D.C. becoming the laboratory for pet congressional education projects. Equally true, however, is the fact that those voucher programs and charter schools were for a long time the only lifeboats D.C. parents had. But his point about black children not relying on a good teacher? It's hard to imagine explaining that to black parents in Boston, Houston, and New York, who had neighborhood schools that were far from perfect but were unlikely to set their children years behind, as they did in the nation's capital. Still, in D.C., teacher quality remained a tough sell, in part because it was a new message—certainly not one they read about in the local newspaper. *The Washington Post* reporters served an admirable oversight role reporting on the corruption, incompetence, and decay in the school system. But nonfunctioning boilers and uncounted students were not the core problems with D.C. schools. The core problems were school leadership and teacher quality.

THE NEW BROOM

Who would be crazy enough to try to turn this mess around? Keeping Clifford Janey, the superintendent at the time, was never an option for Fenty. Janey had done some good things, such as ushering in the Massachusetts standards, but in the minds of the radical reformers who had suddenly seized control, Janey was a slow mover. Adrian Fenty wanted a game changer, someone who would make the most of the freedoms that come with the absolute mayoral control he was insisting on.

Victor Reinoso, deputy mayor for education, and his key staffer, Abigail Smith, were in charge of the search. The buzz in the local press was that Fenty was going to "steal" Rudy Crew, who was running schools in Miami-Dade County. Crew was a big name in urban education, having previously served as chancellor of schools in New York City. Fenty, Smith says, seemed interested in Crew. "But Crew was an urban superintendent, which means that he does what urban superintendents do when they hop from city to city. He had made some noise and done some bold things, but we wanted to look outside that."

. . . . .

That April, NewSchools Venture Fund, an education reform group that applied venture capitalist philosophies to school reform, held its annual meeting in New Orleans. The Fund is primarily known for underwriting groups that spin off high-performing charter schools, such as Uncommon Schools, Green Dot Public Schools, and Achievement First. Attending the meeting were plenty of veterans of Teach for America, which also receives support from the Fund. For someone like Abigail Smith, a former TFAer, a NewSchools Venture Fund gathering is a relief. She was accustomed to attending conferences where Teach for America veterans got cold-shouldered. Teacher union traditionalists, many of whom graduated from state university programs that turn out huge numbers of teachers, take exception to the "elitist" notion that freshly minted graduates from selective colleges can step in and make an immediate impact in only two years. That's just not how teaching works, they insist.

There was none of that attitude at the NewSchools meetings, however. "You go to NewSchools and it's a love fest, because they all did TFA," Smith says. It's the kind of gathering where you could draw a roomful of the nation's top school reformers at an odd hour to brainstorm the impossible: what would it take to save D.C. schools? That's the topic Smith got scheduled for 10 p.m. but it started late, a time TFA founder Wendy Kopp considered impossibly late. But she came, as did many of her superstar peers.

Smith posed the question: Mayor Fenty has just seized control of schools. What does he do and who should he pick as leader? Understandably, everyone at that meeting was tired. "I am not a night person," said Kopp. "I was about to fall asleep." The best brains were tossing out ideas but even the cutting-edge ones seemed dull. And then Michelle Rhee weighed in. Few remember the exact school reform formula Rhee offered near the midnight hour. What everyone does recall was her boldness. At the night grew ever later, Kopp finally gave into her fatigue but before leaving the meeting she leaned over and wrote these words on Smith's notepad: *How about M Rhee?* Smith whispered to Kopp, "Would she do it?" Wendy wrote back: *I think possibly yes.* As she was leaving the room, Kopp whispered to Smith, "Michelle has an iron will." Smith was intrigued. "Wendy's phrase has stuck with me ever since: 'Michelle has an iron will.'"

Equally intrigued was Smith's boss, Victor Reinoso. The next day Reinoso happened to be sharing a cab with Rhee and Smith and used the occasion to toss out a few names as possible candidates. Then he popped his question: "Is this something you would consider?" Rhee laughed and answered, "I'm not your person." Smith and Reinoso, however, were not discouraged. The discussions continued. Over dinner with Reinoso one evening, Rhee suggested people she thought could do the job, including Kent McGuire, dean of Temple University's education school, and Dave Levin and Mike Feinberg, the KIPP founders. "I didn't know if they would do it," she said, "but they fit the profile of who the mayor was looking for." As for considering the job herself, a school super-intendency was "the last thing in the world I wanted." Reinoso insisted on setting up a meeting for the following week with the mayor, which Rhee agreed to, but not to discuss being the chancellor—only to talk about The New Teacher Project and getting better teachers into D.C. schools.

Before Reinoso could tell Fenty about Rhee, the mayor called him and said, "What do you know about someone by the name of Michelle Rhee?" Fenty, it turned out, was responding to a parallel push, this one sparked by Kopp, to lure Rhee into the job. After that meeting in New Orleans, Kopp couldn't stop thinking about Rhee coming to D.C. On an impulse, in the middle of a staff meeting at her New York headquarters, Kopp e-mailed Joel Klein with a simple message: *What do you think about Michelle Rhee for D.C. schools chancellor?* She had dropped the seed and it fell on fertile ground.

·····

Klein, New York Mayor Michael Bloomberg's choice of a game-changing schools chief, was someone untainted by incrementalism, where yesterday's failures are merely tinkered with in slow motion. (Among school reformers, *incremental-ism* is a curse word. It's why Fenty never considered keeping Clifford Janey in the job.) Fenty trusted Klein. He had proved to be an invaluable ally, hosting the entire D.C. city council during a road trip designed to determine whether mayoral control of schools was a good idea. During that visit, Klein knew exactly which buttons to push. When the D.C. council arrived, Klein told them that poor black kids in New York were about two years ahead of poor black kids in D.C. This is not about poverty, he said; this is about school quality and teacher quality. After Klein's sell, the D.C. council voted 9–2 to hand over the school keys to Fenty.

After that vote, Fenty immediately got back to Klein. What should my school reform blueprint look like? Klein advised him to first find the leader, then worry about the blueprint. Fenty asked for names and Klein thought it over. Most of his ideas were what you might call aggressive improvers, people who would take a near-dead school system and make it better. Rudy Crew topped the list. Then Klein got Kopp's e-mail. In a crazy way, it all made sense. The woman who had successfully faced down the fierce Randi Weingarten over unproductive New York teacher work rules clearly had the guts for the job. The question, Klein and Kopp agreed, was how to convince Fenty to gamble on a relatively unknown, thirty-seven-year-old Korean American woman who had never run a school district and was understandably resistant to do so.

Klein called Fenty. He said he had two people. The first, he said, was the safe bet. The second was the "change agent." "She is going to do things that are drastic and fast and cause a lot of controversy," Klein said. "That's the person," Fenty replied. "I want to meet her right away."

Rhee was scheduled to meet with Fenty, and she knew the mayor wanted her to consider the job, but accepting the job still seemed impossible. She had two kids, a home in

Denver, and marital problems. The day before the Washington, D.C., interview, Rhee discussed the job offer with her estranged husband, Kevin Huffman. "He said Washington, D.C., is one of the most screwed-up school systems in the country and very few people could do this—and that I was one of them," she recalled. "He said he would be willing to move to Washington with the kids." Rhee was momentarily stunned. Suddenly, becoming the D.C. schools chief was possible. But did she want the job? And did Fenty really know what he was getting himself into?

. . . . .

Fenty wanted a shroud of secrecy over the interview process so he arranged for Rhee to enter the Wilson Building—Washington, D.C.'s equivalent of city hall—at night through a side door so she wouldn't have to sign in. Rhee found the secrecy humorous. Nobody knew who she was. "They could have me sign in fifteen times and nobody would think anything of it," she said. The meeting resembled a ping-pong match. The more Rhee told Fenty that he didn't really want her—she would be too hard core and controversial for any politician hoping for reelection—the more he insisted that's exactly the kind of change agent he was looking for.

The next morning, Rhee caught a 6 a.m. flight back to Denver to be there for Olivia's graduation from preschool. When she landed, she turned on her phone to find a message from Klein, who had received an early-morning call from Fenty saying, She's the one.

Rhee was intrigued by the challenge but still wondered if she should take the job. Then she talked with John Deasy, who at the time was superintendent of schools in Maryland's

Prince George's County, next door to D.C. She told Deasy she was worried that she didn't know Fenty well enough. "How do I know if he's the real deal?" she asked. Deasy responded, "What do you mean you don't know if you can trust him? This man has staked his entire political career on fixing the school system. He is betting his life on you." Over dinner with Kati Haycock, a national school reformer who founded The Education Trust, Rhee listed the reasons why she should take the job. "I've spent my whole life lamenting the crap public school districts aren't doing, and now I can put my money where my mouth is." Rhee said Haycock played devil's advocate with an answer that would prove prophetic: "The racial politics are going to be insane. You are going to get slaughtered."

Rhee then met again with Fenty. "I told him he didn't want me for this job," Rhee recalled. "He said he did and that's when he impressed me. He said he had no greater aspiration than being the best mayor of the city he could be but D.C. can never meet its potential until the schools are fixed. He didn't care about the politics or pushback. It wasn't going to faze him. As long as I fix the schools, he would be 100 percent behind me." She accepted. Relating this story three years later, she said, "This man has never wavered from what he originally committed."

The announcement was set for June 12, 2007, a Tuesday. To introduce Rhee, Fenty had scheduled a background meeting Sunday at the Wilson Building with *Post* editorial writer Jo-Ann Armao and *Post* reporter David Nakamura. When Rhee walked in, Fenty, Armao, and Nakamura were already talking. When Rhee began to speak, she recalls seeing puzzled faces and realized that Fenty had been talking about other issues without yet disclosing her nomination. Armao and Nakamura had no idea who this unknown woman was, so Rhee had to introduce herself. It was an awkward way to arrive in town. Rhee said that Armao would later tell her that her first thoughts from that meeting were, "Adrian Fenty has lost his mind."[8]

In a meeting late Monday timed to preserve the surprise announcement, Fenty introduced Rhee to Vincent Gray, the council chair who would later emerge as a Rhee critic and successfully run against Fenty. "That was sort of odd, too," Rhee said. "You could tell he was very taken aback as well." More than three years after that meeting, here's how Gray recalls meeting Rhee, as reported in *The Washington Post*:

Gray (D) hoped that the council vote three months later in favor of mayoral control of the District schools would set the tone for a close "partnership" with Fenty (D), one in which the two branches of the District government worked closely on many of the mayor's priorities.

Instead, Gray said his relationship with Fenty was "dealt a blow" even before the school-reform bill became law. On the night before it was to take effect in June 2007, Gray said Fenty walked in his office shortly after 11 p.m. with "this lady." That "lady" was Michelle A. Rhee, and Fenty told Gray that she would be introduced as the new schools chancellor in the morning.

"I was just stunned and like 'How could you do it this way?'" Gray recalls. "When the paper came out the next morning, it was clear *The Washington Post* knew before I did. It was a bit offensive to feel he could trust the media more than the council.[9]

Even more last minute and seemingly off-handed was the announcement to the other councilmembers. They weren't informed until just before the press conference when Rhee entered a breakfast meeting and introduced herself. The most prominent memory Rhee has of the press conference was listening to a *Washington Examiner* reporter "scream" at the mayor for giving the *Post* advance notice about the appointment. It all seemed surreal.

· · · · ·

After the announcement, Rhee visited the central office and promptly carried out her first (of many) firings: Janey's top two aides. Following that came school visits, including the infamous visit to Slowe Elementary, where Tim Daly spotted the sign, *There is nothing a teacher can do to overcome what a parent and a student will not do.* During the next three years Rhee would come to realize that attitude was not limited to the staff at Slowe. "There are hundreds of great teachers in this city, so I wouldn't say *everyone* believed that," she said. "But it was a pervasive mentality, absolutely."

In the central office, that mentality flourished, among other dysfunctions. During breaks between meetings Rhee would wander the hallways and drop in on workers unexpectedly. Rhee would ask what did they do and invariably they would answer with their title. No, Rhee would protest. Not your title. What do you *do* here? The answer was always the same: What my supervisor tells me to do. "They couldn't actually tell me what they were responsible for," Rhee said. "I went up to one lady who said she was in charge of enrollments. I said, 'Great—you are one of the people I want to talk to here. How many students are enrolled?' She started telling me all the complications of why she couldn't tell me." When Rhee hired her data chief, Erin McGoldrick, they discovered the school system used twenty-nine different data systems. "None of them could talk to each other," said Rhee, "and not one was populated with accurate data." Two years passed before Rhee's team was able to cobble together even a rudimentary data system that produced useful and reliable numbers.

The worst central office disaster was the special education operation, which was so incompetently run in 2007 that it sucked up $203 million a year and comprised 20 percent of the school budget. Philadelphia, by contrast, spent 12 percent of its budget on special education; Pittsburgh, 14 percent. Over the years, platoons of outside lawyers had found an easy mark in the DCPS special education system, whose paperwork deficiencies allowed the lawyers to win court orders that sent students to expensive private schools. In some instances parents from other states set up shell addresses in D.C. just to take advantage of the chaos to win private placements for their children.

Rhee appointed her close friend and fellow TFA alum Richard Nyankori to sort it out. One day he came to Rhee with the name of a midlevel special education worker who had failed to fill out the correct forms, resulting in the district having to pay for two $227,000-a-year private placements. "I was appalled and wanted to meet the lady," Rhee said. "So Richard calls her to set up the meeting—but she said she would first have to check with her supervisor. Richard told her, 'The chancellor is your supervisor; she's everybody's supervisor.'" Eventually, they met and Rhee demanded to know why she had cost the district schools a half-million dollars in private placements. "She said that I needed to know that she was a very busy person with too much on her plate and sometimes things fall between the cracks." After the meeting, Rhee told Nyankori to fire her.

In only a few weeks, the firings began to stack up and the department's general counsel advised her to knock it off. Why? demanded Rhee. They're incompetent! The answer: Welcome to District of Columbia Public Schools, where we never fire anyone. Incompetence, it turned out, usually was not enough. The only way anyone got fired, he explained, was to get caught hitting a kid (on videotape . . . multiple witnesses were insufficient) or get caught stealing money. The only way to fire anyone for incompetence, he said, was to prove a recurring pattern. But no one in the central office had been evaluated in years, so there was no way to prove a pattern. So what, Rhee asked the counsel, do you do with central office employees who are impossibly incompetent? His answer: You send them to the schools. "I was like, are you kidding me?"

For a short-term solution, Rhee kept several bad employees on the payroll but didn't let them come in to work. The woman who did the special education paperwork wrong? "My best cost-cutting measure was to send her home," Rhee said. "We sent a fair number of people home." This sent a message to the other workers who barely knew what they did all day: this crazy lady means business.

For a longer-term solution, Rhee went to Fenty for help. His answer: "If you don't like the rules of the game, you change the rules." With Fenty's help, on January 8, 2008, the D.C. Council approved a law on a 10–3 vote making the non-union central office workers "at-will" employees. This meant Rhee could fire whomever she wanted and create a "culture of accountability," as she called it. Over the coming months the firings picked up. "People thought that was going to be it; that was my big thing," Rhee said. And it *was* big: after three years, according to Rhee, the central office wound up at nearly half the size it started. For some new schools chiefs, that would have been enough. They tend to arrive in a city, execute one major change and then hunker down to avoid the incoming flak. Unable to carry out a second big thing, after a short tenure they depart. In Rhee's case, the central office firings were only the first of many firestorms—and, in perspective, the least controversial.

THE RHEE TEAM

To fight the battles ahead, Rhee drew together a team unlike anything seen before in an urban school district. The core was a band of TFAers like Rhee: Kaya Henderson as deputy chancellor; Deputy Mayor Reinoso's former aide Abigail Smith to handle school "transformation"; Jason Kamras, former national Teacher of the Year—who won that award while teaching in Anacostia's Sousa Middle School—to construct the all-important teacher evaluation system called IMPACT, which was designed to both guide and evaluate teachers; and Nyankori got the thankless job of taking on special education.

The first four years of reform targeted two priorities: *human capital*, the bureaucratic term for putting effective principals and teachers into schools, and special education. To the public and press, Rhee's reforms were all about teacher quality. Who's she firing and hiring today? Inside DCPS headquarters, however, the obsession with cracking the special education dilemma cost volumes of sweat and blood. Every Wednesday, when I parked myself outside Rhee's office door and awaited for her to emerge for another "SUV interview," she'd be inside her office grilling Nyankori and others on how to set right a system that was wrong for students and horrifically wrong for D.C. taxpayers.

· · · · ·

Rhee leaned most of all on a tiny group of personal friends who would often go out to dinner with her and hear the first airings of fresh ideas: Nyankori, Henderson, and office scheduling guru Shawn Branch, the Radar O'Reilly of DCPS. To her harshest critics, who viewed all D.C. issues along racial lines, Rhee had a "white" agenda, dedicated to luring more white parents into the public school system. To those who know Rhee, that was laughable. In her day-to-day world, her closest friends, including those three and her fiancé, former NBA star and Sacramento Mayor Kevin Johnson, were black.[10] And her agenda remained the same as when she was teaching in a Baltimore classroom: give more low-income black children a shot at a future.

Outsiders drawn to Rhee's against-the-odds campaign would assume significant roles. James Sandman left a top-flight Washington, D.C., law firm to become her general counsel and retired Brigadier General Anthony Tata got the job of handling logistics for Rhee after returning from duty in Afghanistan. As interim chief academic advisor, California-based education consultant Michael Moody shaped overall strategy. Joshua Edelman (a later hire), who was in charge of reinventing schools in Chicago, came on board to do school innovation for Rhee. Erin McGoldrick, the former data whiz for the California Charter Schools Association, would prove to be a ruthless numbers gatherer for Rhee, sorting out the scores of data systems that didn't overlap. At times, Rhee had to order McGoldrick to go home: it was too late to be working. And she drew on trusted insiders as well, such as Lisa Rudin, her chief of staff, who had worked with Rhee at The New Teacher Project. Rudin managed the talent across departments.

It was, to say the least, an unprecedented gathering of national education talent. During the summer months, when there were no SUV interviews available, I would drop in for every-other-week talks, often while Rhee enthusiastically consumed another of her famously carbo-loaded lunches. The only time I saw her completely lose focus on her food was the day I gamely asked her if she would swap her staff for the deputies who served Secretary of Education Arne Duncan. Presumably, Duncan had the pick of the land. She almost choked on her meat loaf: not a chance.

• • • • •

To see what made her advisors special, start with James Sandman, a legal advisor who knew how to help her get where she wanted to go. In October 2007 Sandman was a corporate litigator and former managing partner for Arnold & Porter, one of the nation's elite law firms. After thirty years as a lawyer, as he was finishing a term as president of the D.C. Bar, he began to think about taking on a public service role, probably at the federal level. And then he was invited to a breakfast meeting of the Lawyers' Committee for Civil Rights and Urban Affairs at the Grand Hyatt in Washington, D.C, where the featured speaker was Michelle Rhee.

"She arrived after the breakfast had started," Sandman said, "and I was immediately impressed. She arrived alone. No entourage. I don't think she was even carrying a purse. Most people in her circumstance don't go anywhere alone. They have someone to show them where to go, carry their bags. She got up to speak and just blew the room away. She conveyed passion and energy and a can-do attitude. She did it all with a big smile on her face, communicating optimism and enthusiasm while not downplaying the magnitude of the obstacles she faced."

At the end of the speech, Rhee rhetorically asked what the lawyers could do to help. After ticking off three of four actions, she unexpectedly added, "Does anyone know where I can find a good general counsel? I need one. I'm surrounded by lawyers who only know how to say 'no.'" Immediately, Sandman thought: "I want to work for her."

He went home and asked his wife, who responded, "You need to take this job." "My kids thought it was interesting, too," Sandman said. "For them, Michelle Rhee was kind of a rock star."

Sandman applied for the job. One of his interviews was a come-ride-with-me-I'm-running-late interview when he ended up observing Rhee conducting a meeting at a school. "She was fielding all kinds of questions from an audience that wasn't very happy about an action being taken," he said. "She was very direct. She didn't tell people what they wanted to hear but she answered every question honestly. She didn't take any notes but seemed to remember what each person said."

Rhee offered him the job and he left Arnold & Porter. Some of his law office partners got it, others didn't, and you could tell right away just from their faces who was who, he said. "Some thought it was the greatest thing in the world; others, I could tell, wanted to say how sorry they were for me." Sandman, however, was just where he wanted to be, helping Michelle Rhee figure out how to get a legal "yes" for the reforms Michelle Rhee needed most.[11]

· · · · ·

Kaya Henderson, another of Rhee's closest advisors, grew up in Mount Vernon, New York, where she attended public schools, except for a short stint in a Catholic girls school. In high school, she was a "traditional overachiever," she says—senior class president, captain of the cheerleading squad, and an athlete, playing on the basketball and softball teams. Much of her drive may have come from her mother, a teacher and the first person in her family to go to college. She was the kind of mom who insisted her daughter take Latin, not keyboarding. Henderson, who was offered a full scholarship to attend Harvard University, instead chose Georgetown University, where she graduated from the foreign service school.

Henderson was accepted by Teach for America and assigned to teach Spanish at a middle school in the South Bronx, about four miles from where she grew up. "I was twenty-two and I thought I could change the world," she said. Henderson had started studying Spanish in third grade and studied abroad in Spain, Venezuela, and Mexico. Unlike

Rhee's initial experience, Henderson's first year was smooth, possibly helped in part by the fact that Spanish was an elective the students didn't need to graduate. "Mostly what I did were games and songs and chants. Kids liked my class because it was fun." The South Bronx may have been close to Mount Vernon but there were important differences between her students and how she was raised. "My students were as smart as we were," she said, "but they lacked parents who could actually advocate for them, parents who knew what their children should be getting and demand that they get it. Most of the experiences these parents had with school were bad."

After two years of teaching Henderson became a TFA recruiter, inspired by what she had seen the four TFA teachers in her school accomplish. "The level of energy and commitment my TFA colleagues brought to the kids was transformational to both the students and the culture of the building," she said. Soon, Henderson rose to director of admissions at TFA, responsible for bringing in new corps members, five hundred at a time. "I managed the largest group at TFA and prior to that I hadn't managed myself out of a paper bag," she said, laughing at the memory. "In that job I learned probably half of what I know about managing people." After more than two years on that job, Henderson ran the TFA operations in Washington, D.C., for more than three years. "At that point I had been with TFA for eight years," she said. "I felt like there had to be a world outside the cult."

She planned to attend graduate school to gather the credentials needed to become an urban schools superintendent. Already she had one big question on her mind: Why isn't everyone emphasizing teacher quality? Those plans were interrupted by a phone call from Rhee: Come work for me at

The New Teacher Project. Teacher quality is our sole focus. Plus, I'll offer you a $25,000 raise. "I was like, 'School and debt, or a job with a raise?' I'll go with the job!"

For the next seven years she worked for TNTP. Because one of Henderson's responsibilities was managing the D.C. Teaching Fellows program, which had been established in 2000, Henderson became an expert on how the city's hiring operation worked. It wasn't pretty. "I lived through countless HR directors," she said. At that point Henderson, who was looking for a new challenge, entered a graduate program at Georgetown University. But once again, Rhee, who was on the verge of accepting the job as D.C. schools chief, intervened.

On the day before meeting with Mayor Fenty, Rhee called Henderson. If I take this job, Rhee said, you have to promise to come work with me. "I need you to bite off your pinky," Rhee told her. Whenever there was a huge commitment that needed to be made at The New Teacher Project, Michelle would tell this story about medieval Korean warriors who, when they were taking a serious oath, would bite off their pinkies and sign their names in blood. Henderson protested, saying this was not a pinkie moment, because Rhee would not become chancellor. "You're going to say no, they're going to say no to you," she told Rhee. Just in case the improbable happens, Rhee insisted, give me your pinkie oath. Henderson did.[12]

· · · · ·

Hires such as Henderson and Abigail Smith gave Rhee—an outsider, technically—expertise on the D.C. school system. Smith could immediately take over on school closings. She knew it cold. And Henderson, who had spent years dealing with teacher and principal hirings at DCPS, knew exactly where the bodies were buried. She also knew, in advance, just how horrendous the central office was. Her perspective, however, is slightly different from Rhee's. The problem wasn't the employees, but the people who had ostensibly led them. "If you know you have too many people and you're not evaluating out incompetent people, it's not the fault of the incompetent people," she said. "Most had never gotten any feedback. They were not asked to act any differently. It wasn't their fault . . . but they still had to go."

There was urgency in the air and not much time. Who better to bring in to take over the logistics than a brigadier general? Typically, when a retired military officer plunges into a school district the idea is to impose martial discipline on unaccountable schools and unruly students. That formula rarely works out. What do generals truly know about educating urban children? In this case, however, the general's assignment was at the heart of his expertise: logistics, exactly what he did for the 10th Mountain Division in Afghanistan. The legendary chaos within DCPS didn't faze Tata, a West Point graduate. "I'm used to making order out of chaos," he said.

Actually, Tata felt at home with the clear-cut reporting system he found. The spokes of the D.C. reporting system were superintendents who oversaw principals who oversaw teachers—akin to an Army chain of command in wartime reaching out to forward operating bases. In Afghanistan, the key was getting to know the officers who ran the forward operating bases. Same with schools. Mimicking his methods in Afghanistan, Tata drew up a map that documented his school visits to meet with school principals and building business managers. And he instituted a predictable communications system akin to what he used in the battlefield. "We established what in war was called the operations sync meeting," he said. "Every day you have a battle update brief, where everyone around the country comes online for an hour, and every commander would give an update on his or her status. Everyone is listening. I wanted to do something similar, because for an hour a day you were focused and you had your whole team there, and you could put out any message you needed."

In D.C., the sync meet was weekly rather than daily: every Wednesday from 1 to 2 p.m., with eighty to ninety people on the call, usually school business managers, who talked about everything from food delivery to paying coaches. To Tata, schools have resource issues that differ only slightly from what forward operating bases demand. Instead of bullets-and-beans questions, schools ask about technology needs. But everybody, in combat or classrooms, complains about the food.

Fixing the food problem—both the cost and quality— was Tata's biggest challenge. Overseeing a $28 million food contract with 122 sites, his goal was to start shifting from one large supplier to multiple suppliers offering healthier foods. The district committed to buying more local produce and getting rid of milk flavored with high-fructose corn syrup. To Tata, improving food service was directly connected to Rhee's goal of boosting student performance. "I want to be able to put some wind behind her sails by saving money that can be plowed back into academics," Tata said. And he knew that 70 percent of DCPS children lived in poverty and hungry kids don't learn.

Tata was impressed with the unique talent he was able to recruit to DCPS. He drew a technology person from Wall

Street, a food services director who had run a Manhattan restaurant, and a former Army captain from the 82nd Airborne
to handle logistics. They told him straight off they were
drawn to the jobs because of Rhee. Tata says a lot of people
wanted to work for him because they wanted to "touch the
Michelle Rhee magic." [13]

Chapter Five

CLOSING SCHOOLS

There is a scene in *Waiting for "Superman,"* the Davis Guggenheim documentary released in fall 2010 that follows several inner-city children desperate for a decent education, in which a tight-lipped Michelle Rhee is surrounded by red-faced protesters shouting their outrage. She doesn't move, doesn't change expression. Many interpreted that impassionate stare as arrogance, which only heightened her growing reputation as the Queen of Mean. Undoubtedly, that impression drew strength from Western stereotypes of Asians as emotionless and calculating. That segment from *Waiting for "Superman"* was shot during the school closing hearings in early 2008. "There are a lot of clips of me at the end of these meetings where people are literally screaming and they have signs saying, 'Rhee Must Go!'" she said. "I attended hundreds of meetings in that time period and everywhere I went it was the same thing over and over again: 'You don't care about our kids.' 'This will be horrible.' 'Smaller schools are better for our kids.' I was called every name in the book, things were thrown at me, people picketed my office. It was intense."

In 2010, long after those meetings, Rhee smiles about the emotionless shots from the film. "I guess I didn't look concerned enough." So what was going through her mind as the protesters were yelling and screaming? "I kept thinking that what had happened in this school district for years was crazy. Look at the outcomes! So you can yell at me all you want, but this isn't going to happen under my watch. This is why [previous superintendents] didn't close schools. It's an exhausting process and you get screamed at. If you are a sensitive person, and you take this all personally, then you waver over closures."

Prepping for Surgery

Crazy is not a hyperbolic description of the bloated facilities Rhee found when she arrived. There had long been D.C. schools that need closing—yet nobody bothered. For years, officials spent massive sums of money on an aging, sprawling infrastructure while students departed for private schools, charter schools, or the suburbs. In 2001, DCPS had sixty-six thousand students, while eleven thousand went to charters. During the next eight years, the size of DCPS fell to forty-five thousand students, while the charter school population rose to twenty-eight thousand. The dollars that should have been going to the children who remained instead were spent on maintaining too many boilers and painting too many lightly used hallways. At the time Rhee arrived, for example, DCPS had 101 elementary schools but needed only 86 to serve both current needs and future expansion. The district was losing $18 million a year on food service—an area that should be profitable, given government reimbursements—because too many buildings housed too few students, so resources were spent needlessly trucking food around the city.

Though the source of the problem was clear, with a school board and city council willingly held hostage to groups dedicated to preserving the status quo, it seemed impossible to close unneeded schools. Why take the heat? But everything changed in 2007 when Mayor Fenty seized control of the schools. Now, a schools chief could properly downsize absent political meddling. It had to be done. "You can't operate efficiently when there are only ninety kids in your school," said Rhee.

The question wasn't whether to close schools, but how. Fenty had very strong views. He realized there was no easy way to do it. The Rhee team planning the closures settled on three operating assumptions. First, you can involve people all through the process, but no matter how you slice it, many will be unhappy—so you may as well pull the bandage off quickly (Fenty's suggestion). Second, don't present the public with hypothetical school closings and invite a wave of early criticism. Rather, develop the criteria for closings, identify the schools, and present the public with a complete plan. Third— and this proved to be the really tricky one—don't indulge in symbolic political closings. If some city wards have more underused schools than others, so be it. Take the political heat and close the schools that need closing. (That last point is the kind of sentiment that goes over better in a private conference room than a public community meeting.)

. . . . .

In those early days, Rhee was scrambling to get the inner workings of DCPS on track. Although she would assume the public face of the closings, much of the behind-the-scenes work fell to Abigail Smith and Eric Lerum, chief of staff to the deputy mayor for education, Victor Reinoso. Lerum had arrived in D.C. in 2000 to enroll in law school at American University, when he participated in a fellowship program that taught constitutional literacy to students at a charter high school for public policy. He started out with no interest in or knowledge of education. But, Lerum said, "pretty early on I started to feel a connection among education, civil rights, justice—all the things I was interested in." After law school he worked for the D.C. State Board of Education for two years, developing education policy. When Fenty won the mayor's race, Lerum joined Reinoso's staff.

On the question of why the bloated school infrastructure was allowed to persist, Lerum declines to point a finger at either previous Superintendent Clifford Janey or the school board. "Janey had to report to nine board members and get change and reform through nine people," he said. "They weren't bad people or incompetent, but they are nine different people and you had to have to have their sign-off on every decision. Boards have a habit of wanting to micromanage." That changed, Lerum said, with the mayoral takeover of schools and Rhee's "drive and determination and the contagious atmosphere that she creates with her leadership team."

Together, Lerum and Smith pulled together the previous studies and plans for streamlining the district, including one put together by Janey. Smith said Janey's administration mapped out closing twenty schools over thirteen years. "The direction that we got from Michelle was that we were not dragging this out," Smith said. "We were going to close a whole bunch of schools in one fell swoop and take our medicine." Several think tanks had already done the heavy lifting, including a ward-by-ward, building-by-building analysis of underused capacity. Lerum and Smith worked to assemble a list, as quietly as possible. "The longer you give people to react ahead of time, the more time they have to fight you," said Lerum. "We wanted to come up with a plan that made sense and then have people react. If you give them something half-baked, it would get mired in debate."

The process moved quickly. The closing criteria became obvious—all you had to do was look at a ninety-student school like Slowe Elementary. Although schools with dwindling enrollments during the previous five years were the primary targets, that wasn't the only consideration. "Just because the data tells you the school is empty doesn't mean it's in the best interest of that neighborhood to get rid of that school," Lerum said. "It might make sense to close a couple of schools around it and rebuild that school. In late November 2007 it was announced that twenty-three schools would be closed, for an estimated savings of $23.6 million a year. In theory, that money would shift from maintaining empty hallways to educating children. Saving money was a key factor, but instructional concerns mattered, too. "If you spread all the kids out, it's hard to offer quality programs," said Lerum, referring to an obvious professional development challenge of spreading teacher-training capacity. Mile wide, inch deep is a formula guaranteed to bleed resources.

Best Laid Plans . . .

The announcement was choreographed down to the second, with the council chairman to be briefed first thing in the morning and the affected principals informed just after that. To say that it didn't work out as planned would be an understatement.

As Smith tells the story, a mole from the Office of Public Education Facilities Modernization ("I have my theories on who, and yes, that person still works there") leaked a school closure list to *The Washington Post,* which on November 28, 2007, published a story on the closures. It wasn't the final list but it was accurate enough to do damage. A public relations disaster ensued. The principals didn't know why they had been summoned to the central office and so were blindsided when they saw the newspaper. Councilmembers, too, learned about the closures from the press rather than the administration. And because the *Post* published a list that wasn't entirely accurate, some communities were misinformed about their school's closure. "We were pissed. The mayor was pissed," Lerum said. "We were fighting a story that was [in part] the wrong one."

Things only got rockier in the days after the botched announcement. A blizzard of meetings followed, some of them overseen by Smith and Lerum, others by Rhee, many by both. It didn't help that the trio in charge of closing schools that served nearly all black students consisted of two whites and a Korean American. Sometimes minority members of the DCPS staff would show up for the hearings but for the most part it was Lerum, Smith, and Rhee taking the heat. Race was always an undercurrent. "It was usually subtle," said Lerum. "It was 'You don't understand us or our kids or our schools.' And they would attack us for being from 'out of town.' You would hear a lot of, 'I don't care where you come from; you don't understand how important this school is.'"

Ward 5 in the northeast, represented by Councilmember Harry Thomas, was set to lose five schools, the most of any ward.[1] Bunker Hill Elementary had a 2006 enrollment of 246, a decline of 42 percent from five years previously. Enrollment at Slowe, with its eighty-three students, had fallen 64 percent. The reasons for the enrollment declines might have been clear—the primary culprits were an aging population and the rising popularity of charter schools—but the closings didn't go over well. Thomas himself started taking heat, despite the fact he wasn't consulted on the plan. When he tried to calm an unruly crowd questioning Rhee at one Ward 5 town hall meeting, he drew boos. One parent holding a toddler daughter jumped up and said, "You didn't listen to us! Did you call me? Did you ask me?"[2]

Thomas introduced legislation to give the council authority over the closings but it was too late. The council had already turned over control of the schools to Fenty, who in turn vested Rhee with near-total freedom to turn around a persistently failing education system. This was Rhee's call—and burden. The fact that Rhee's team never informed Thomas of the proposed school closings, especially considering the number of schools targeted in his ward, was a slight he would never forget. Later, Thomas became a strong supporter of Vincent Gray's challenge to unseat Fenty. "That was huge for me," he later said.

· · · · ·

For Rhee, Lerum, and Smith, the hardest part of the school closings wasn't the angry councilmembers or yelling parents. It was watching parents during the school-by-school closure hearings try to protect schools that had failed their children, and in many cases, themselves. It was painful exhibition of the D.C. phenomenon expressed in the Slowe sign: principals and teachers were doing their best with the children who showed up on the doorstep. Hearing that message from parents was difficult; it showed how deep the pessimism had reached. These were their own children they were talking about.

For Lerum, the saddest case was M.M. Washington High School in Ward 5, a school where in 2007 only 33 percent of the students were proficient in reading and 20 percent in math. Lerum will never forget the visit he and Smith made to the school. "The building had no windows and most of the kids were just congregating in the cafeteria, but not for an assembly or event," he says. "They were just there hanging out, being rowdy and doing nothing. No adults were doing anything. No one asked us a question as we walked through the building. This was a high school, supposed to be a career high school. It was just dirty and dark and no learning going on. We walked out of there fighting the feeling that we had to go back into the school and do something right then."

Rhee's saddest case was Draper Elementary, a Ward 8 school that only had about one hundred students. In 2007 a little more than half the students were proficient in reading, only a fifth in math. Prior to the announcement, Rhee arranged to meet Councilmember Marion Barry at the school. Barry was late, a habit he is known for, so Rhee walked across the street to a housing project. "There were these middle-aged men sitting there, and they were like, 'It's a great school, and we don't need another boarded-up building in this neighborhood,'" she recalled. "But it was not a good school. The proficiency rates were ridiculously low. The sad thing is there was a KIPP charter school two blocks away where 90 percent of the kids were proficient. It was sad because it showed the disconnect about this school. The principal had been there for like thirty years, so there was this sense of security because they were all good people. But nobody was looking at it to see if the kids could read."

Smith shares the sentiment: "To have parents defending these schools was kind of heartbreaking. It wasn't because their kids were getting fabulous educational experiences. . . . It was because that was their neighborhood school; it was where they went and their parents went. All those are valid and strong personal feelings. I'm not dismissing them. But to hear people really advocate for these schools that were serving kids so poorly was a difficult thing to hear in this process."

As an example, Smith points to P.R. Harris Educational Center, a school in Anacostia for pre-K through eighth grade. In 2007, only one in five children at Harris read at grade level. "This was a really low-performing school and parents were talking about how safe their children felt there, that they have wonderful teachers. This school had been a dumping ground for horrible teachers for years. There were several schools that were the last schools in line for teachers on their way out and P.R. Harris was one of them." At the closure meeting, the Harris parents would not acknowledge the failings of their neighborhood school. "The parents would say that people could say what they wanted about Harris, to them it was a wonderful school," Smith said. "But by any objective measure, it was a terrible, failing school."

· · · · ·

Smith's experience on Deputy Mayor Reinoso's staff meant that she knew all sides of D.C. school politics—so she was hardly naive about the risk Rhee and her team took by not informing the council of the closures well in advance of the announcement. Councilmembers were not happy to have been blindsided. "For the council, this was their first experience of 'whoa . . . this lady is not playing around and this is for real,'" Smith said. "It was right there in their face."

Lacking the buffer of a school board, which had been disbanded, the councilmembers were left feeling the heat. They had to choose: would they start acting like a school board and try to reassert themselves or would they honor the power they granted Mayor Fenty when they unanimously voted to cede him control of the schools? Not surprisingly, several councilmembers chose the former. Smith recalls one who in private readily admitted the need to close a cavernous, underused school in his ward. But on meeting day, he rose to incite the parents in protest. "He said one thing from one side of his mouth to the chancellor but he was at every community rally inciting the crowd."

It was too late though. The council could posture and try to save face but there was no way to retract the vote to give school reform authority to the mayor. In truth, they didn't really want to be accountable for D.C. schools; they just wanted to deflect the political heat to Rhee. For the most part, they succeeded. And as always, Rhee paid a price: one more uptick in unpopularity.

Fait Accompli

Among the early decisions made about closures, the one that caused the most trouble was the decision to avoid "political" closings. As it turned out, the schools located in prosperous

Ward 3 were jammed with students. Still, closing just one school in the nearly all-white Ward 3 might have greased the skids to closing five schools in the nearly all-black Ward 5. Says Lerum: "Every councilmember brought up that a school should be closed in every ward. It wasn't based on what was right for kids but rather their idea of fairness or whatever."

Rhee held her ground, despite the heat from Councilman Thomas, who was shaping up as her harshest critic. She brought him a spreadsheet showing that even if all the planned closures went through in his Ward 5, it would still have the most school square footage per student. She says he told her, "I notice you aren't closing schools in Ward 3 because you like white people." "And I said 'No, it's because schools in Ward 3 are bursting at the seams.' They have the lowest square footage per child and they are all high-performing schools. Why would I shut them down?" Thomas denies making the comment about Rhee favoring whites.[3]

The school closings only marked the beginning of strained relations with the council. In hindsight, Rhee's options were limited. Had Rhee's team publicly announced the need to close schools and then invited comment, they would have been bombarded with not-in-my-neighborhood protests and the council might have mustered veto authority. Few if any schools would have been closed. But going out with a complete plan, as they did, invited the you-didn't-consult-me protests. Smith said that if they were to do it again they'd seek comments on the criteria for closing schools, though not the list of schools. "Of course, if you do that, a smart reporter would still figure out what schools would end up on the list." Rhee estimates that she did more community engagement meetings on school closures than any other issue but concedes she is remembered as the emotionless autocrat who rammed the closures through while accepting little input.

The smart move by the Rhee team was deciding to move quickly. Fenty's bandage analogy proved to be the wisest: tear it off quickly and completely. "Even when you try to engage everyone, school closures make people unhappy," said Rhee. "It's better to have them unhappy for a short period of time than a long period of time." The unexpected lesson from the closings is that once the bullet is bitten, closing more schools becomes easy. Since the furor of the initial closing, DCPS has shuttered schools each year on a much smaller scale. No furor. One of the closings didn't even make the papers.

. . . . .

Successfully closing twenty-three schools in one clean and relatively brief attempt was an impressive feat. "Nobody closes twenty-three schools, nobody," said Smith, shaking her head in amazement. But the job was hardly complete. In 2010, Anthony Tata, Rhee's chief operating officer in charge of logistics, was asked to take a few days to serve as part of the evaluation team for the five school districts that had emerged as finalists for the 2010 Broad Prize in Urban Education. Tata was assigned to the team evaluating Gwinnett Public Schools just outside Atlanta. Almost immediately, something caught his attention: Gwinnett had 110 schools serving 155,000 students. By contrast, District schools had 45,000 in 123 schools. More schools for far fewer students, and this was *after* Rhee forced DCPS to close twenty-three schools. Unfortunately, numbers like that failed to convince D.C. communities. Not only did people think Rhee was arrogant and spurned advice, they thought she favored the white, middle-class schools in

Ward 3. In Washington, D.C., where all political events are carefully weighed by race, that last perception inflicted the most damage. The fray also marked a schism between Rhee and several key members of the council.

The question about school closings is no different from other controversial decisions Rhee made. Was there a "nicer" way to do it? If she had just smiled and collabo-rated, could she still have closed twenty-three schools? "I think you could have," says Thomas. "You sit down with the parents and get some buy-in." Rhee's staff disagrees. The only certainty here is the political damage inflicted. From that point forward, critics such as Harry Thomas, Vincent Gray, and Marion Barry would begin to mimic the role of the school board they had abandoned And that would come back to haunt both Rhee and Mayor Fenty.

Chapter Six

RANDI AND MICHELLE

The education field rarely produces outsized personalities, probably the result of risk-averse school boards weeding out fiery school leaders early. The same is true at the federal level, where secretaries of education generally are nice, smart, and soporific. Take President Clinton's secretary, Richard Riley. Nicest guy ever and guaranteed to put you to sleep five minutes into a speech. Current Education Secretary Arne Duncan is considered "interesting" because he's tall and occasionally plays basketball with the president. That's how low the bar is set. Margaret Spellings, the education secretary under President George W. Bush, was considered something of a wild child because she wore hip Marian-the-Librarian glasses and occasionally unleashed Texasisms such as "put on your big-girl panties and deal with it." Crusading education reformers, the very people you'd predict to be interesting extroverts, in fact tend toward being painfully earnest and awash in jargon. Most days they gather on Andrew Rotherham's Eduwonk Web site where every Friday Rotherham does his best to inject some color by running a "fish porn" feature with photos of education wonks holding their catches.

That's what made the Michelle Rhee–Randi Weingarten clash so compelling: two truly outsized personalities bristling with willfulness, intensely aware of their places in history, and unwilling to back down when their core values were at stake. Rhee and Weingarten, regardless of sharing Cornell University as an alma mater, truly dislike one another—none of that posturing you see in the Senate, when at one moment two members are thundering at one another, the next they're chummy at a Capitol Hill softball fundraiser. "You have two strong-willed and very smart and determined women with very different agendas," Chester Finn Jr., a former assistant secretary of education and a senior fellow at Stanford's Hoover Institution, told *Newsweek*, "It has an almost gladiatorial aspect to it."[1]

· · · · ·

The Rhee-Weingarten showdown in Washington, D.C., caught both women at critical times in their careers. Weingarten was freshly arrived in D.C. as president of the American Federation of Teachers after years spent in New York as president of the United Federation of Teachers, where she successfully defended the UFT's considerable power base in New York. Plus, she had been semisuccessful at repositioning her union as part of the solution rather than part of the problem. Weingarten was doing her best to assume the senior statesman role achieved by the highly regarded late AFT president and reform advocate Albert Shanker. Weingarten, however, was not fortunate enough to live in Shanker's time, when a teachers' union leader just talking a reform line was sufficient to earn accolades. Weingarten lived in a time when the society was saturated with news about America's declining K–12 schools. She faced a panoply of challenges around the country: charter schools eager to hire nonunion teachers, legislatures increasingly willing to blame union work rules for the sorry state of their schools, and an openly skeptical press that in 2010 extended to cinematographers unflinching in their portrayals of teachers' unions as the villains that were denying poor children a shot at the American dream. Just listen to the menacing music that arises when Weingarten appears on the screen during *Waiting for "Superman."* This was a pivotal time for Weingarten, whose union represented the urban districts under attack: would these unions endure as political playmakers or get pushed aside by governors winning votes by promising to turn around persistently failing schools? Pressuring Weingarten from the opposite direction were her union members living in tough economic times: teachers were in no mood to give up their hard-bargained job protections, even the over-the-top ones that embarrassed the unions when described in newspaper articles.

For Rhee, the stakes were equally high. Mayor Adrian Fenty had staked his political career on tapping the relatively unknown Rhee as the change agent who could solve the one remaining puzzle that kept Washington, D.C., from becoming a first-class city—schools that rose above the level of national embarrassment, a threshold previous mayors and schools chiefs had failed to cross. Given that most of Rhee's reform strategy in D.C. revolved around achieving a sharp boost in teacher quality, that meant winning radical changes in the ways teachers were hired, evaluated, professionally developed—and fired. All that came down to a simple mandate: win a new teachers' contract that in years past would have been considered not just unwinnable but a complete and utter fantasy. Given that Rhee was the new kid on the block, compared to the streetwise Weingarten schooled in the sharp-elbow politics of New York, that seemed a long shot, at best.

IN THEIR WORDS

Each of these gladiators possessed unique powers of persuasion and matching toughness. Rhee wasn't a crier; neither was Weingarten. Understanding their power requires a look at their core values as revealed in their speeches. A typical Weingarten speech reiterates the harshest complaints made about teachers unions; a Rhee speech reiterates the sorry state of student learning when she arrived in the district. Here's part of Weingarten's speech to the AFT annual convention in July 2010 in Seattle:

> I stand before you today sure in the knowledge that we have examined our policies, looked at our practices, and made changes when we've needed to change. That has sometimes been hard, but it gives us needed credibility to hold a mirror up to others.

> But frankly, I am shaken to the core—in fact, I am horrified—by the immense threats to public services, particularly public education, that exist in the corridors of power in this country. I suspect many of you in this hall feel the same way.

> I never thought I'd see the superintendent of a major city's public school system call public education, and I'm quoting here: "crappy."

I never thought I'd open a major newspaper to see us described as (again I'm quoting): "self-interested adults trying to deny poor parents choice for their children."

I *might* have expected to hear the House Republican leader say that preventing teacher layoffs is a scheme to, quote, "pad the education bureaucracy."

But I never thought I'd see a Democratic president, whom we helped elect, and his education secretary applaud the mass firing of 89 teachers and staff in Central Falls, R.I., when not a single one of the teachers ever received an unsatisfactory evaluation.

And I never thought that I'd see a documentary film about helping disadvantaged children in which the villain wasn't crumbling schools, or grinding poverty, or the lack of a curriculum, or overcrowded classrooms, or the total failure of No Child Left Behind.

No, the villain was us.

Look, I can take it. It's part of my job.

But taking abuse shouldn't be in the job description of more than 3 million public school teachers who work hard every day to do right by their students.

. . . The blame-the-teacher crowd would have Americans believe that there is only one choice when it comes to public education: either you're for students, or you're for teachers.

That is a bogus choice.

When a school is good for the kids, it's also good for the teachers, and vice versa. And if our leaders fail to recognize this, and fail to create a positive vision for our schools, we must lead the way.[2]

Following is an excerpt from Rhee's speech when she accepted an award in 2009 from the John Glenn School of Public Affairs at Ohio State University:

Let me first start by giving you a little bit of background about the city and school district when I came into this job a few years ago. At the time we were largely known as the lowest-performing and most dysfunctional school district in the country. We were the only school district in the country on high-risk status with the Department of Education, mostly for the misuse of federal funds. We had an achievement gap in this city, between where the white students were performing and the black students were performing, of 70 percentage points. . . . If you were a ninth-grader in one of our comprehensive high schools in this city, you had a 9 percent chance of graduating from college. And . . . only 8 percent of our children were operating on grade level in mathematics. Eight percent. Which means that 92 percent of our kids did not have the skills and knowledge necessary to become productive members of society.

And perhaps the most disheartening data was about our little ones. And basically what that data said was that when we got kids into the system in kindergarten, they were essentially on par with kids who looked like them in other cities across the country. So, not with their suburban counterparts, but with kids who looked like them in cities like Philadelphia, Dallas, Houston, San Francisco, across the country. The problem was that the longer they stayed in our school district, the further behind they fell, so much so that by the time they were in the third grade they were far below their urban counterparts.

And this was an interesting statistic, which is that by the time our children reached the fourth grade, they were in a position where the poor black fourth-graders in New York City were operating two full grade levels ahead of the poor black fourth-graders in Washington, D.C.

So for everyone who wanted to blame the low academic levels of our children on single-parent households and the poor neighborhoods and lack of health care and all those things, what I said was that the last time I checked, the poverty in Harlem did not look all that different from the poverty

in southeast Washington, D.C., but the kids in
Harlem are a full two grade levels ahead of our
kids. So basically, what I meant was that if you are
a kid in this system, you are essentially better off
staying at home every day than you were coming
to school, where you would fall further and further
behind. That was the reality.[3]

. . . . .

To Weingarten and other AFT officials, Rhee headed a parade
of opportunistic "reformers" who cynically pretended that solving America's urban education problems was as simple as sweep-
ing out bad teachers. What made Rhee more dangerous than
other reformers, they thought, was her uncanny ability to convince others, especially the national press, that the truth was on
her side alone.[4] The real Michelle Rhee, the AFT team thought,
was a naive player out of her league who needed to be reined
in. To Rhee and her supporters, Weingarten was someone who
over the years had said one thing and done another so many
times that she had lost a grasp on what constituted the truth.
During a panel discussion on NBC about *Waiting for "Superman,"* that attitude spilled out on national televisions as Rhee
told Weingarten: "You cannot say that you support removing
ineffective teachers, when I fire ineffective teachers and then you
slap me with the lawsuits and you slap me with the grievances."

The setting for the confrontation was Washington, D.C.,
a tricky place for Weingarten to orchestrate a battle. This was
the nation's capital, which guaranteed national attention. If
Rhee got what she wanted, every school board in the country
would be demanding the same. Worse, the local AFT chapter,

the Washington Teachers Union, had been weakened by scandal. A recent president, Barbara Bullock, was in jail for embezzling union funds.[5] Bullock's replacement, George Parker, is a big man with a booming voice and a viselike handshake. But the cliché "appearances can be deceiving" applies here. Parker was forced to constantly look over his shoulder as his vice president, Nathan Saunders, challenged his every move and vowed to oust him from the presidency. All that made Parker a jittery bargaining partner to Weingarten (and Rhee). Rhee had her own handicaps to deal with in D.C. Forcing the closures of unneeded schools saved money and tightened academic controls but also generated a small army of Rhee critics, ranging from councilmembers who felt they had been thrown under the train to parents who felt that their voices meant nothing. Regardless, the stage was set and the match would be fought in Washington, D.C.

Most viewed Weingarten and Rhee as first crossing swords over the D.C. teachers' contract but insiders knew that their first confrontation occurred in 2005 in New York when Rhee, then a relative nobody heading up The New Teacher Project, agreed to testify on behalf of then–New York Chancellor Joel Klein over sensitive work rules. Given the power wielded by the unions, nobody else volunteered for that assignment . . . except Rhee. But in any power game, measuring winners and losers is tricky. Klein and Rhee won the battle that day but the confrontation only girded AFT leaders for the war. When Rhee was appointed chancellor in Washington, D.C., in 2007, some AFT officials in D.C. recalled that New York hearing as though it happened the day before. Payback, as the cliché accurately points out, can be hell.

· · · · ·

A moment for rapprochement between Weingarten and Rhee arrived in summer 2009 when it was clear that Weingarten was about to be officially appointed AFT president. The proper thing to do, a Rhee advisor counseled, was to arrange a "kiss the ring" meeting with Weingarten. Reluctantly, Rhee agreed, but she came to regret it. Weingarten basically said, according to Rhee, "Clearly, you've made a lot of mistakes, and clearly, you are not going to want to do any of that now that you have this important job." Rhee held her tongue and tried to be nice.[6] Soon, rapprochement would become impossible. Rhee stopped by a New Schools Venture Fund annual meeting in Washington, D.C., at just the moment Weingarten, speaking on a panel, attacked a research paper from The New Teacher Project that found that many of the "excessed" teachers in New York—teachers unwanted at local schools but kept on the payroll as per the union contract—weren't even looking for new teaching positions. That report, said Weingarten, was "jerry-rigged" and "almost completely flawed." Rhee was astonished that no one in the audience was challenging Weingarten. When Rhee couldn't hold it in a moment longer, she stepped up to a microphone to correct Weingarten, who held her ground. The exchange, Rhee concedes, was "catty."

There was no middle ground in this clash, as Rhee moved quickly to secure an innovative teachers' contract, one that would evaluate teachers based in part on how much the children in the classroom learned, an approach that continues to be regarded around the country as somewhat exotic. The best teachers, Rhee thought, should earn the top salaries, the worst teachers should get pink-slipped immediately, and the weak teachers should get extra help—and then be fired if they fail to improve. Rhee's goal, putting an effective teacher in every classroom in every ward of the city, sounded altruistic, but in D.C.'s case, by my estimation, it meant flushing out huge numbers of teachers, those who, even with steady infusions of professional development, would never scrape D.C. schools off the pavement. Not until all classrooms had decent teachers could the district push the accelerator on sophisticated curriculum reforms used successfully in other urban districts.

The likelihood of Rhee succeeding was slim: no schools superintendent anywhere in the country was dismissing more than a handful of teachers for ineffectiveness. Regardless, Rhee concluded, it had to be attempted. Making Rhee's challenge even more difficult was the fact that her team couldn't hope to match the decades of contracting negotiating experience and talent Weingarten and her team could bring to bear. Rhee's top negotiators, deputy chancellor and longtime friend Kaya Henderson and former teacher of the year Jason Kamras, who designed the IMPACT teacher evaluation system, had impressive urban education credentials. But when it came to high-stakes collective bargaining, they were innocents. Not only were they innocents but their proposed contract represented an existential challenge to Weingarten and the AFT. If the union couldn't protect their members' jobs, what was the point of having a union?

The Red and the Green

Not intimidated by the mismatch, Rhee bolted out of the negotiating gate immediately with a contract proposal that quickly became known as "red and green." Teachers choosing the red track would continue professional life as usual, and those opting for the green track could earn higher salaries if they proved a higher level of effectiveness. The trade-off for the green-trackers: they had to relinquish some tenure protections. The plan was bolder than any schools chief had ever offered. "If Rhee accomplishes this, it would be earthshaking reform that would have implications everywhere," Bryan Hassel, codirector of Public Impact, an education research and consulting organization in Chapel Hill, N.C., told the *Post*.[7]

To encourage more teachers to embrace the green track, Rhee secured commitments from several foundations to pump millions of additional salary dollars into the system. That was an eye-popping carrot and in spring 2008 Rhee was close to convincing Parker to put the plan to a vote. At that point, Weingarten and the AFT were mere bystanders—alarmed by what Parker appeared to be giving up, but bystanders nevertheless. Much to Weingarten's relief, that union vote never happened. On July 3, 2008, the *Post* printed an article that undoubtedly frightened a lot of teachers. The headline said it all: "Rhee Seeks Tenure-Pay Swap for Teachers."[8] Although the article later explained the distinctions—that teachers had the "red track" option of retaining seniority—the *Post* article, according to Rhee, was enough to cause an anxious Parker to back off: no vote.[9]

That article, says Rhee, probably postponed the contract by nearly two years. At the time, she was furious. In hindsight, however, it proved to be a godsend. For teachers mostly worried about retaining their jobs, that red-green contract offering was an excellent deal. If teachers had approved that contract and then chosen the red track en masse, Rhee's reforms would have suffered an early death. She might as well have resigned in embarrassment. "If you really wanted to screw me," she says she told Parker at one point, "what you should do is sign the contract and tell all your members to stay on red, because they would all get a pretty significant bump in pay and nobody has to change seniority rules.

· · · · ·

At this point in the 2008 contract negotiations, momentum lurched in a very different direction. At the request of the Washington Teachers Union board, the American Federation of Teachers was officially invited in as partner negotiators— "advisors" would be the public line. Although Weingarten was always very careful to publicly remind everyone that these were Parker's negotiations, no one was fooled. This was now Weingarten versus Rhee. Weingarten couldn't stand that Parker almost gave away the store. She assigned her top negotiator, Rob Weil, to oversee the day-to-day machinations. A former math teacher in Douglas County, Colorado, Weil negotiated the progressive teacher quality contract there that linked teacher pay to student performance. That gave him the kind of Al Shankerish credentials Weingarten cherished. Although Weil took over the day-to-day burden, Weingarten was never far away. The nation's eyes were on this contract.

During the next year, the contract morphed into a power struggle between Rhee and Weingarten. On January 31, 2008, the AFT scuttled the entire red-green concept by countering with a nuts-to-bolts counteroffer that didn't even acknowledge Rhee's original reformist intentions. Rhee's team scraped themselves off the ceiling and kept going. Both sides endured scores of late-night meetings and dozens of offers and counteroffers, all of which went nowhere. In spring 2009, both sides agreed to a mediator, former Baltimore Mayor Kurt Schmoke. What followed was a year of hush-hush negotiations patiently presided over by Schmoke.

THE STORYLINE SHIFTS

Here's where the story took an interesting twist. In hindsight, it seems clear that what was happening in the negotiations behind closed doors got eclipsed by other dramas playing out within D.C. over teacher firings and nationally over a strong surge in teacher-quality reforms. The D.C. drama kicked off in October 2009 when Rhee unexpectedly announced the firing of 266 teachers. The City Council changed the budget numbers, she said, which left her no choice. The layoffs proved to be a public relations debacle for Rhee. Not only did councilmembers dispute the numbers but the council and Washington Teachers Union demanded to know why she had hired an unusually large number of new teachers, more than nine hundred, only a few months earlier. Rhee must have known about the upcoming budget change, they charged, which gave her an excuse to fire teachers she wanted to get rid of anyway.[10]

Things only got worse when Rhee gave an interview to *Fast Company* magazine that included this quote: "I got rid of teachers who had hit children, who had had sex with children, who had missed seventy-eight days of school."[11] For Rhee haters, and there were a growing number, the careless language was a gift, and the *Post* Metro section willingly served as megaphone. Not only had Rhee plotted to fire older teachers, the critics said, but now she also was broad brushing laid-off teachers as sex offenders and child abusers. (Eventually she would clarify that since July 2007, she had fired only ten teachers for corporal punishment and two for sexual misconduct.) In hindsight, of course, it is easy to observe that there was nothing very controversial in the *Fast Company* quote: she did get rid of teachers who had hit and were child abusers. But that's irrelevant. What matters is how it was interpreted at the time.

What really heated up the firing controversy, however, was Rhee's refusal to fire by seniority: last hired, first fired. Instead, she asked principals to recommend which teachers should be let go based on their performance. That's when all hell broke loose. In Rhee's words:

> It outraged the unions—and not just the teachers
> union. At a rally in D.C.'s Freedom Plaza—fully
> outfitted for the occasion with a stage, lighting,
> and port-a-johns—the leaders of the Washington
> Teachers Union and the American Federation
> of Teachers were joined by Richard Trumka of
> the AFL-CIO. They denounced us for making
> children victims and guinea pigs. A few thousand
> demonstrators showed up, some of them holding
> signs with statements like "This is not Rheezistan,"
> accusing us of tyranny and union busting.
> Hundreds of school districts across the country
> were laying off teachers at the time, but the union
> establishment protested en masse only in D.C.,
> where for the first time someone dared to question
> an entrenched practice that had only served the
> interests of adults.[12]

That was Rhee's lowest point at the helm of D.C. Public Schools. The firings, which inevitably involved mostly black teachers (unavoidable, considering that most teachers in D.C. are black) gave Rhee's critics an opportunity to start portraying her reforms as racially biased. The controversy over the quotes in the magazine article made her look like she was accusing the fired teachers of being child abusers. Worse, the firings severely disrupted the talks over a new teachers' contract. Who wants to negotiate after an in-your-face mass firing? Completely lost in the jumble of controversies was the core issue: Rhee had let principals choose their low performers, thus breaking the last-hired, first-fired barrier. This was when she most needed someone like Secretary Arne Duncan to stand by her side and point out what all the shouting had obscured: many of those fired teachers were low performers who needed to be removed.[13] But Rhee made the federal officials nervous. Their strategy with the unions was to sweep them up as reform partners, forcing them to dance along as partners. The whole partner strategy wasn't working all that well—the two national teachers unions allowed their disdain for Duncan's reforms to spill out in public. But that was Duncan's strategy and he was sticking by it. Rhee, by contrast, was more the stand-and-deliver type. Definitely not a dancer.

In many school districts, a public relations disaster of this magnitude would trigger an immediate and cold dismissal. But Fenty stood by Rhee and over time the firing controversies paid off for Rhee in two ways. Not only did releasing weak teachers give Rhee more opportunities to find stronger teachers but the firings ended up helping get the contract approved, according to both Rhee and AFT negotiators.[14] Rhee may have been taking a public relations battering, but D.C. teachers saw another message in the firings. "It made the rank and file realize they did not have the protections they thought they had," said Rhee. "It made them feel, 'Oh my God, this woman is willing to go further than anybody else. She's not playing around.' They thought, If this is going to be reality, then we might as well get some money, too." Months later, after the unintended benefit became clear, Rhee was asked if she planned it all along. "I'm not that smart and strategic. It just happened to have helped us."

THE NATIONAL SCENE

The second development that eclipsed the private negotiations emerged on the national scene: governors and a handful of big city schools chiefs started demanding teacher-quality reforms—work rules, tenure reforms, and performance pay—that previously would have been considered politically impossible. No doubt, some social scientists claim to know exactly why certain issues suddenly pop to the surface of the nation's psyche to become everyday concerns. To me, the actual reasons why teacher quality, Rhee's core reform philosophy, suddenly became a mainstream issue the public "got" will remain a mystery. It just did. The proof lies in hundreds of news articles around the country honing in on that exact question. Absent this rethinking of the teaching profession, the eventual contract Rhee won in spring 2010 would have been a long shot.

Teachers, unlike most U.S. workers in the private sector, are rewarded not for effectiveness but for time served and graduate degrees earned, a formula that guarantees odd outcomes. Washington State, for example, discovered that despite years of national debate over the need to attract higher-quality math and science teachers with better salaries, those teachers were, on average, earning less—the result of fewer years on the job than the social studies and gym teachers.[15] And teachers, also unlike most U.S. workers, almost uniformly get top job ratings regardless of their performance. As Rhee often repeats in her speeches, when she arrived in D.C. just 8 percent of the school system's eighth-graders were proficient in math, 12 percent in reading—and yet 95 percent of the teachers received satisfactory or better ratings.

To noneducators peering in from the outside, the nearly ironclad job security teachers enjoy is striking, especially in comparison to their own jobs. Even for extreme offenses, such as sexually abusing children, teachers rarely get fired. Instead, school districts often end up offloading those teachers onto unsuspecting districts, as a 2007 Associated Press investigation discovered. And if teachers rarely get fired for major offenses, you can imagine how few get fired simply for being ineffective. Until Chancellor Joel Klein began trying to fire bad teachers in New York City, few school chiefs even thought it was possible. But even a push by Klein produced little: between 2008 and 2010, Klein was able to fire only three teachers for incompetence.[16] Since 2000, Los Angeles school district officials have spent $500,000 per teacher trying to fire just seven of the district's thirty-three thousand teachers for poor classroom performance. Of these, only four were fired. One was reinstated and two of three were paid large settlements.[17] Principals in Portland, Oregon, reported that attempting to fire just one teacher takes an extra five to ten hours *every week*, not to mention the emotional drain of ongoing contentious battles with the teachers and their union representatives. The incentive, then, is to strike a deal with a bad teacher, either outright or through coercion: leave my school and I won't fire you.[18]

Weingarten has an explanation for ineffective teachers: sure, there are bad teachers just as there are bad architects and lawyers. That sounds logical but only at first glance. Anyone working in a free-market job knows what eventually happens to incompetent architects and lawyers. Too many flawed buildings, too many bungled legal cases . . . they lose their jobs. It's only a matter of time. Not so with teachers. When Rhee took over the D.C. schools in 2007, the district was tied with Los Angeles as the worst in the country. And yet not a single teacher in the previous year had lost his or her job because of ineffective teaching.

Around 2007 everything changed, all due to that mysterious "pop" in public perception. Across the United States, reform-minded school chiefs suddenly realized they had a green light to tackle what in years past was a no-go issue. In 2009, when Rhode Island education commissioner Deborah Gist ordered superintendents to stop basing school assignments on teacher seniority (a system that usually left the neediest schools with the least effective teachers), she won national applause while the union merely cringed. Then, in 2010, when she fully backed the firing of all the teachers at persistently failing Central Falls High School, she not only won the public approval of President Obama but also was named to *Time's* 100 Most Influential People. The unions were apoplectic but they had to see this coming.[19] Louisiana's Republican governor, Bobby Jindal, launched a broad assault on nearly everything held dear by the Louisiana Association of Educators, proposing more charter schools, teacher evaluations tied to test scores, and an end to teacher tenure and seniority privileges. Colorado legislators overrode strenuous union objections to impose a bill that stiffened the threshold for achieving tenure and made it easier for teachers to lose it.

Even Hollywood got into the public opinion shift. During summer 2010, four documentaries emerged that drew national attention to the plight of U.S. urban schools. In each, the unions played the villain role. For teachers, who over the years have nurtured an apple-on-the-desk image, this had to be painful. The most prominent film was *Waiting for "Superman."* In this, Rhee plays a star role. The title refers to poor, urban families waiting for a Superman to rescue their children, either a Rhee-type crusader or a high-performing charter school willing to take them in. Although AFT president Randi Weingarten gamely attended the film's opening in Washington, D.C., she seethed about its anti-union message.[20]

TIME TO VOTE

Amidst all these highly public battles, the quiet negotiations overseen by Schmoke eventually wrapped up. On June 2, 2010, Washington, D.C., teachers ratified a new contract by a vote of 1,412 to 425. It would be a mistake to suggest this was a resounding vote of confidence for Rhee, who remained deeply unpopular among many teachers who despised the new reforms, especially the IMPACT evaluations. For the most part, the lopsided vote was hunger to get a paycheck for three years of back raises and in part an acknowledgment, given the dramatic shift in popular opinion, that Rhee's reforms were unstoppable. After the vote, mediator Kurt Schmoke said as much. "The ideas have gained currency at the national level," he said. "What was seen as bold is now reform, not revolution."[21]

So who won, Michelle or Randi? After the contract was approved, each spoke carefully measured words, insisting that her side walked away with its core values intact. The only real way to answer that question is by actions: did the contract in any way limit Rhee's reforms going into the new school year? It would appear that just the opposite played out; the contract accelerated her reforms. That year, the pay-for-performance plan kicked in, the key tool she planned to use to lure effective new teachers and convince the best teachers to stay. On September 10, Rhee issued $45 million in retroactive pay increases that affected more than 650 educators who rated "highly effective" on their IMPACT evaluations. On the other side of the ledger—removing weak teachers—in summer 2010 she terminated 165 teachers for poor performance and put another 737 "minimally effective" teachers on notice that they would be terminated within a year if they failed to improve.

The biggest breakthrough was the end of "forced placement," where teachers whose jobs were eliminated by, say, reforming a failing school were owed jobs elsewhere in the system. When Rhee reconstituted Dunbar High School in 2008–2009, for example, and the takeover team unearthed evidence that the counselors there had failed to keep their students on a path toward graduation, those counselors were forced out of Dunbar—but not fired. According to the contract, Rhee had to find jobs for them elsewhere. As a result, one hundred Dunbar teachers, counselors, and other staffers had to be dispersed among other schools—schools already in academic trouble. "Instead of hiring the crackerjack people they believe in," Rhee said of principals receiving those teachers, "they get the ten from Dunbar who were forced on them." Not so after the new contract. When Rhee began to reconstitute Ballou High School at the end of the 2009–2010 school year, 40 percent of the teachers were let go. Of those, only eight were rated "effective" teachers and even those eight were not guaranteed jobs in other schools.[22]

. . . . .

Does that mean Rhee "won" her battle with Weingarten? She forced ineffective teachers out of the system—a first for D.C. And she created a salary incentive system to retain the best teachers who in the past often gave up on the system and moved to more comfortable suburban districts. Rhee placed D.C. Public Schools at the nation's forefront of education reform: if any failed urban school district could be turned around, this appeared to be the one. Measured in a broader way, however, the contract she "won" was just another nail in Fenty's political coffin, ensuring Rhee's departure. "The racial politics will kill you," Rhee was warned when she considered taking the job. True enough. As the mayoral election would soon reveal, the firings were viewed by many in racial terms. As election day approached, polls showed that Rhee was seen positively by only a quarter of the African American women in D.C. The very mothers who had been damaged by bad schools when they were growing up and whose children were being harmed in exactly the same way turned against Rhee and her reforms.

Only on the surface is that illogical. These women had no way of knowing that D.C. teachers were placing their children two years behind similar children in other cities. Nobody had ever told them that. They lived in economically beleaguered neighborhoods where the school system was seen as a steady source of employment for adults. To many, the Slowe sign made sense: first, solve poverty; then expect improvements in academic achievement. Seeing their neighbors, relatives, and friends get fired from teaching and classroom support jobs, one of the few avenues to a middle-class life, didn't go down easily. Worse, in this one-news-source-town these mothers had reason to believe the teacher firings were random rather than based on ineffectiveness—no more than a "spin of a roulette wheel" wrote one *Post* columnist.[23] There was a price to be paid, and on primary day, September 14, both Fenty and Rhee would feel the wrath.

Chapter Seven

NEW HIRES, NEW FIRES

The school district Michelle Rhee inherited in 2007 was in freefall. Not only had student enrollment plummeted and test scores scraped the bottom of any national rankings, but also many principals had lost control of their schools. Rhee's response to the latter was to eject (or offer voluntary retirement to) nearly fifty principals who had tolerated those conditions.

Her yardstick for progress was basic. In the first year, a principal entering an out-of-control school must succeed in "locking down" the school: seize control of the hallways, bathrooms, lunchrooms, and the nearby city blocks during school dismissal and ensure calm and respect in the classrooms. If principals succeed with that first-year lockdown but test scores still look miserable, they generally got a pass.[1] The second and third years, however, measurable "teaching and learning" was supposed to kick in. If that didn't happen, the principal was "nonreappointed," the district's euphemism for getting fired. Not surprisingly, a lot of principals stumbled along that path, which means a lot of nonreappointments—and a lot of interviews for new principals. Given the challenges, one might assume aspiring principals would have steered clear of D.C. but that was not the case. The excitement stirred by Rhee's reforms triggered a surge of applicants from would-be principals seeking to prove themselves in tough conditions under a national spotlight.

But finding the right principal to turn around a troubled school is an art. Talented educators who might be stars in other school districts, even some gritty urban districts, often wilted under Rhee in D.C. "Our principal recruitment is good and our pool is large," Rhee said. "Our problem is that we have extraordinarily high standards." As many as one thousand candidates applied each year Rhee held the chancellorship. Anyone seriously in the running was interviewed by Rhee herself. "Within three minutes, I can tell if that person would make it," she said. "It drives me nuts. They will say something like, 'It's all about data-driven decision making,' and when I ask what that means they will give me a blank look. They know the buzzwords but not what is beyond that. Or I will say, 'Do you think you were successful at your last school position?' and they will say yes. I'll ask why and they will say it's because the parents and students like them and all that fuzzy stuff. At that point I know it's not good." What's good to Rhee? If they arrived at their previous school with 20 percent of students reading on grade level and when they left, the number was 70 percent.

Rhee has done enough interviewing to be familiar with a certain type walking through her door: men who look like a million bucks in their suits. White shirts, red ties, everything a perfect fit. All too often, however, the million-buck suit turns up empty. These guys may talk a good game but they can't quite turn the corner while being peppered by Rhee on how they would drive school improvement. Buttoned into his suit, Dwan Jordon fit that description when he walked in for his interview with Rhee in 2008. But within the first minute, Rhee realized that Jordon was no empty suit. At the time, Jordon, a D.C. native, was an assistant principal at a middle school in neighboring Prince George's County, the suburb where many black D.C. residents end up in when they depart the District for greater safety, better schools, or both.

The strong first impressions were mutual. "She was different," Jordon says, "hard-nosed." The worst-case-scenario question she posed him—"The school you are assigned isn't where it's supposed to be. The kids are fighting, your staff is not on board. Tell me what you would do."—was no hypothetical. On Rhee's arrival, most schools fit that description. In that first interview with Jordon, as she listened to him adroitly explain how to seize control of a school, Rhee knew not just that she wanted to hire Jordon but exactly which out-of-control school he would be assigned: John Philip Sousa Middle School in Anacostia, a school of 267 students that is 99 percent African American with nine of ten students qualifying for free or reduced-price lunches. "I could tell from my conversation that by sheer force of will he would make things happen," Rhee said. "He had a real interest in music and the arts. Sousa had a rich tradition of being an arts school so I knew it was a good fit." Sounds great but consider the odds of Jordon succeeding. Sousa was a contender for the title of the worst middle school in the D.C. system and was located in a neighborhood most white Washingtonians have visited only through crime stories in *The Washington Post*. Anyone who saw *Waiting for "Superman"* may remember Sousa as the school Anthony desperately wanted to avoid as he awaited the charter school lottery results.

WELCOME TO ANACOSTIA

In Tom Wolfe's 1987 novel, *The Bonfire of the Vanities*, "master of the universe" Wall Street bond trader Sherman McCoy was driving from Kennedy Airport to Manhattan, mistress in tow, when he took the wrong ramp and ended up in the Bronx, which resulted in some highly unpleasant consequences. For many white Washingtonians and suburbanites, the *Bonfire of the Vanities* wrong turn happens at the end of the Pennsylvania Avenue bridge that crosses the Anacostia River. Make a left turn at the end of the bridge and you're on your way to your yacht in Annapolis or weekend place on the Eastern Shore. Miss that turn and you're in Anacostia, a nearly all-black neighborhood known to outsiders mostly by headlines—drug deals, shootings, horrific schools, and minor political scandals involving former Mayor Marion Barry. Residents in Anacostia's Ward 8 forgive Barry's transgressions and see him as their hero, in part because they credit him for bringing a Safeway supermarket and other first-world stores to Alabama Avenue.

What few white Washingtonians realize is that Anacostia is hardly a stock movie ghetto with burning tires and roaming gangs. The area is full of very pleasant neighborhoods with immaculately maintained yards. And that Safeway on Alabama Avenue is better stocked than many suburban supermarkets in Washington, D.C. That said, parts of Anacostia at night are every bit as dangerous as the crime statistics make it look and the poverty is appallingly real: unemployment in Wards 7 and 8 can be as high as

25 percent and another 40 percent are underemployed or have given up looking for work.[2]

.....

Sousa Middle School, located in Ward 7, a short drive from the bridge, merits a visit. On a very hot day in late May, I got a tour of the neighborhood from Tyrone Pittman, Sousa's dean of students, the school's discipline enforcer. The school is a National Historic Landmark, nearly as significant in the national civil rights history as Little Rock Central High School. Prior to the mid-1950s, Sousa was an all-white high school.[3] In 1949, a group of Anacostia parents, the Consolidated Parents Group, joined with James Nabrit Jr., a Howard University law professor who would become the university's president, and challenged the separate but equal doctrine, arguing that the D.C. school board should make Sousa an integrated junior high school. The need was especially compelling considering the surge in the D.C. black population, which had doubled in size between 1930 and 1950. During World War II new schools construction had been halted and by 1947 many black children were on double or triple school shifts, while seats in many white schools sat empty. In 1950, the head of the Consolidated Parents Group, accompanied by police and lawyers, showed up at Sousa with eleven black schoolchildren and asked to enroll them. They were denied, which led to *Bolling* v. *Sharpe,* a lawsuit that the Supreme Court decided on May 17, 1954, along with *Brown* v. *Board of Education.* Almost overnight, Sousa flipped from all-white to all-black as white families abandoned Anacostia.

Today, the high ground overlooking Sousa is dotted with scruffy four-story brick apartment buildings. A building across from the school parking lot is used as a halfway house for men rotating out of jail. Further up the hill, many apartments are boarded up. Others lack real locks on the doors. The apartments, which go for about $400 a month, are inhabited by single parents and grandparents and a few kids each. The adults mostly work—some steady jobs, janitorial jobs—nothing good enough to get them out of the neighborhood. If they could afford $1,000 a month in rent, they would probably move across that Pennsylvania Avenue bridge to the North Capitol Street area, where it's slightly safer. To white Washingtonians, both neighborhoods seem equally dicey, but to black residents, a move northwest means a stronger police presence and, in their mind, a better high school. But they don't have that money and probably lack a car. So they stay, with all their earnings going into groceries and clothes. After 8 p.m., they pay a price for being too poor to move. "At night this place is a war zone," Pittman says. "You'll find drug trafficking in the street, gambling. The kids who live here are told to stay in the house after a certain hour." Police come around, yes—after something happens.

Jordon, Meet Sousa. Sousa, Principal Jordan

On July 1, 2008, Jordon arrived at Sousa and started going through the test score data from previous years. "It was horrible," he said. Only 22 percent of the school's three hundred students were at grade level, or "proficient," in reading, and just 16 percent in math. No kids scored "advanced." None of the teachers had been evaluated the year before he arrived. The administrators just never got around to it. "I think it was just too chaotic," Jordon said. He saw the evaluations from the year before that. Most teachers received "meets expectations," and some got "exceeds expectations"—at one of the worst middle schools in one of the worst districts in the country.

One by one, he called in the teachers and each conversation started out with a review of the test score data. At that point, the budget was done and there was little he could do about the teachers who were already there. He was, however, able to hire seven teachers to fill vacancies, two assistant principals, and two instructional coaches, enough to complete a leadership team to set the tone, a very different tone, for the new school year.

· · · · ·

The first goal was to reestablish control of the school, where Jordon was told students felt free to run around, fight every day, even have sex in the building. "Kids were spending more time outside than inside the classroom," he said. Jordon decided students would wear uniforms with clothing subsidies offered. He made sure that was clear in all correspondence to parents and the first day of school only one student showed up lacking a proper uniform. Reclaiming control of the hallways was a more challenging task. "The first two weeks of school were like a boot camp," Jordon said. "I planned out every minute of the day for everyone. When students walked through the door, they were greeted by someone who escorted them to the auditorium, where they sat in a specific section to go over rules. They were walked to class, walked to lunch. Everything was structured. It took us two weeks, but the whole culture changed. People ask me, 'How did you reclaim control of the school so quickly?' I tell them, kids will do what you ask them to do if you are being consistent as adults."

Then came the hardest part: ratcheting up the performance of teachers who had tolerated such miserable student outcomes. Jordon knew that Rhee was building a teacher evaluation system, IMPACT, that weighed student performance at half a teacher's score. IMPACT would be available in a year, but with Sousa's miserable score data, a year was too long to wait. So Jordon figured out a way to use the old system—the system in which 95 percent of D.C. teachers emerged with great ratings and only 8 percent of eighth-graders were at grade level in math. Jordon calculated that there were twenty-eight steps required to flush out a low-performing teacher. Submit improper paperwork on any of the twenty-eight and everything gets tossed.

"When the school year started, to be honest with you, we bombarded teachers with informal observations. We gave them very specific feedback, we showed them what we thought good instruction looked like," said Jordon, such as "differentiated" instruction designed to reach all the students in the class. Some teachers were even given scripts to follow. "The constant informal classroom observations continued for the entire year. Why am I doing that? I have a sixth-grader going to a D.C. public school. My measuring stick is, would I want my child to be in one of the classrooms here? If the answer is no, that's a problem. But that's what I used for a measuring stick. So, some teachers made it, some didn't."

At the end of the year, more than half of Sousa's staff was gone—shown the door by use of an evaluation system that had never truly been used to evaluate, only to issue meaningless praise. Which teachers left? Jordan lists examples: "I walked into one classroom and the teacher was asleep." Fired. "I had another situation in which a teacher had four or five corporal punishment cases for the year." Fired. "I had a veteran who was here for more than twenty years who didn't know how to write an objective. That's one of the first things you learn as a teacher, how to write a goal for your class, how to write an objective that's student friendly." Not invited back. And then there was the teacher he observed teaching a math problem incorrectly. Gone. The rest simply couldn't live up to Jordon's best teaching practices.

William Wilhoyte, who oversees middle schools for Rhee, sees a parallel between Jordon and Rhee. "He went into Sousa the way Michelle came in here," Wilhoyte said. "He had a mandate to go in and do some things and it wasn't terribly democratic. It was, 'This is the way we're going, here's the path, here's the plan, and if you want to be part of it, fine. But if you don't, look out, because I'm coming after you.' We fought a lot of battles that first year, with the union and others saying we were doing things we shouldn't. But we were just holding people accountable and responsible for what they ought to be doing."

· · · · ·

The real gains from Jordon's first year at Sousa came from reestablishing control of the school and hiring seven new teachers from outside D.C. schools. Plus, there's what educators call going after the low-hanging fruit—just teaching students how to take a test, basic things that suburban students already know. Those initial actions were sufficient to produce some eye-opening gains. During Jordan's second year, scores jumped again as he forced more staff changes and continued his tight focus on what good teaching looks like. Between 2007 and 2010, the percentage of Sousa students proficient in reading jumped from 15 to 41; in math, from 14 to 46. Such gains, Rhee said, are "unheard of. This is when I went to the school and it was amazing. Kids were on task, engaged in learning." Jordon was not satisfied, though. "People are like, 'Wow, how did you do it?'" he said. "But I'm looking at it as, we still have 60 percent who are not proficient." Jordon wanted the same number of kids proficient at the middle schools in Anacostia as on the tonier side of D.C., west of Rock Creek Park. "It's no secret," he said. "If you have good teachers, that's half the battle."

At the end of the 2009 school year, Rhee was visiting a nearby elementary school. On leaving at the end of the school day, she happened to drive near Sousa. "It must have been 95 degrees that day and we're driving near Sousa, probably five blocks away, and there's Jordon with his walkie talkie telling everyone to move along," Rhee said. "He was like traffic-copping. I rolled down my window and said this is what I was expecting to see from him. He is out there in his suit and tie sweating and getting the kids to go home and do their homework."

Jordon, Rhee said, is very headstrong. "He alienates some people and I started getting e-mails from people pretty early on that he was not listening to them, that he was acting like a dictator, etc. But a lot of those were coming from the usual suspects, so if he was raising their ire I knew he was doing some pretty good stuff. He moved out more teachers than any other principal did last year.[4] My staff will tell you that his paperwork was better than anyone else's, even though the volume was larger. As many times as I have been in the building I have never seen him in his office. He is always in the hallways and classrooms.

When you watch him walk through the hallways, there are few administrators like him. Nothing goes unnoticed. He is nagging a kid to tuck in his shirt. 'Why didn't you go to practice yesterday?' He isn't a warm fuzzy guy. He is intense. I got an e-mail from a parent that the subject line said 'the warden'—it was about Dwan Jordon. But the parent meant it in a good way."

NEW BLOOD

What Jordon did at Sousa is a lesson on the principle of *snap* I referred to in the preface. He brought in teachers with snap. On the surface, they might look like the teachers from the failure years. But what they do in the classroom is very different, starting with their expectations.

SUNARIA TATUM

In December 2008, Tatum was working in a hospital as a phlebotomist, teaching others how to draw blood. Teaching seemed natural to her; in fact, she had always wanted to be a teacher but her Caribbean family members warned her off. Do something different, they urged her. So she did. After graduating from LaGuardia High School of Performing Arts (think *Fame*), where she was a singer, she left for Western State University in West Virginia, which had offered her a scholarship to study biology. That led to the phlebotomy work but the itch to pursue education never left her and she found she liked teaching at the hospital and decided to pick up her education credentials. Then it was time to decide where to apply for a job. She and her husband had just moved to D.C. and her son was headed into D.C. schools. "I figured I needed to know what was going on before he entered into that realm," Tatum says. "That's why I decided to choose D.C." And Sousa just felt right. "I thought I could make a difference here."

Her break came in January 2009 when another teacher departed and Tatum took over the class, teaching sixth-grade language arts and social studies.[5] Dwan Jordon was looking for teachers who didn't believe there were limits to what they could do with "flawed" children from Anacostia. In Tatum, he found a teacher infused with the West Indian education ethic that sees education as the key to self-improvement. A perfect fit. Tatum had found a home.

Literacy, argues author and curriculum designer E. D. Hirsch, involves far more than merely teaching children to "decode" text, or sound out words, which is the primary emphasis in the early grades of most urban schools. The assumption behind the solo focus on decoding skills is that once children learn the mechanics of reading, they will then absorb the meaning of the written material presented to them in class. The Reading First grant program launched by the federal Department of Education under President George W. Bush operated on that principle, handing out hundreds of millions of dollars in grants to intensify the focus on decoding. It never worked well and the reason, says Hirsch, is that you can't learn reading without context. You can't understand what you read without knowing about the broader world. He offers this example of a young boy in a struggling South Bronx school taking a test:

> The test begins, and the very first passage concerns the customs of the Dutch colony of New

Two-year-old Michelle with her younger brother, Brian, at their Toledo home. *Photo courtesy of the Rhee family.*

Rhee in middle school in Toledo. *Photo courtesy of the Rhee family.*

Teenaged Michelle with parents, Inza and Shang; older brother, Erik, left; and younger brother, Brian. *Photo courtesy of the Rhee family.*

Rhee at her graduation ceremony at Harvard's Kennedy School with friend Layla Avila (May 1997). *Photo courtesy of the Rhee family.*

Rhee with her mother, Inza, and daughters, Olivia and Starr (2006). *Photo courtesy of the Rhee family.*

Press conference as Mayor Adrian Fenty officially takes over the District of Columbia Public Schools (DCPS). He introduces Rhee as the D.C. schools chancellor. Pictured (from left to right): Vincent Gray, D.C. council chair; Michelle Rhee; Adrian Fenty; Jim Graham, D.C. councilmember. (June 12, 2007). © *Sarah L. Voisin*/The Washington Post/*Getty Images.*

Fenty and Rhee paint a stair railing at Drew Elementary School in Washington, D.C. (August 24, 2007). Fenty and some of his cabinet members were on hand to help clean up the school in preparations for DCPS Beautification Day.
© *Ken Cedeno/Bloomberg/Getty Images.*

Rhee, Fenty, and D.C. Attorney General Peter Nickles with students at Payne Elementary (summer 2010). A press conference was held at Payne one month before the 2010 District of Columbia Democratic mayoral primary election.
Photo courtesy of District of Columbia Public Schools.

Time Magazine cover: "How to Fix America's Schools"
(December 8, 2008). From TIME Magazine; December 8, 2008
© *2008 Time Inc. Used under license.*

American Federation of Teachers President
Randi Weingarten (December 2008).
© *Mitch Dumke/Corbis.*

The Senate Appropriations Committee held hearings to address appropriations provided to improve the education of children in the District of Columbia. Testifying were Michelle Rhee; Josephine Baker, executive director of the District of Columbia Public Charter School Board; and Gregory Cork, CEO and executive director of the Washington Scholarship Fund (September 16, 2009). © *Melina Mara*/The Washington Post/*Getty Images.*

District of Columbia teachers protest outside the office of DCPS Chancellor Michelle Rhee over possible layoffs (September 24, 2009). © *John McDonnell*/The Washington Post/*Getty Images.*

President Obama's inauguration, Washington, D.C. Pictured: Michelle Fenty, wife of Mayor Adrian Fenty; Adrian Fenty; Michelle Rhee; Kevin Johnson, Michelle's fiancé, mayor of Sacramento, and former NBA basketball player (January 20, 2009).
© *AP Images/Donna Cassata.*

Washington, D.C. premiere of *Waiting for "Superman."* Pictured: American Federation of Teachers President Randi Weingarten, producer Lesley Chilcott, musician John Legend, Viacom President and CEO Philippe Dauman, filmmaker David Guggenheim, Michelle Rhee, and Kevin Johnson (September 15, 2010).
© *AP Images/David Snyder.*

Rhee announces her decision to step down from her position as DCPS chancellor at a news conference. Pictured: Adrian Fenty; Kaya Henderson, deputy schools chancellor and Rhee's interim replacement; and Vincent Gray, City Council chairman and future D.C. mayor (October 13, 2010). ©*Alex Wong/Getty Images News/Getty Images.*

Washington Post cartoon by Tom Toles, posted the day after Rhee's resignation (October 14, 2010). *TOLES © 2010* The Washington Post. *Reprinted by permission of Universal Uclick. All rights reserved.*

Amsterdam. You do not know what a custom
is; neither do you know who the Dutch were, or
even what a colony is. You have never heard of
Amsterdam, old or new. Certainly it's never come
up in class. Without background knowledge, you
struggle with most of the passages on the test. You
never had a chance. Meanwhile, across town, more
affluent students take and pass the test with ease.
They are no brighter or more capable than you are,
but because they have wider general knowledge—as
students who come from advantaged backgrounds
so often do—the test is not much of a challenge.[6]

Tatum gets that, which is why she pushes so hard to give
her students a broader connection. "I know from the beginning
that my kids are going to have problems with informational
text," she says. "Why? Because they are not prone to reading
the newspapers; they are not prone to watching the news. They
are not prone to looking at biographies or reading any types of
autobiographies. They are prone to the Internet and BET and
things of that nature." Her children don't live in a text world,
so she finds ways to bridge the gap. The lesson on the day I
visited, for example, was on character development—a concept
her students do not know from books. "So I stop and say, 'Has
anyone seen *Malcolm in the Middle*? Yes? Great. Okay, so that's
a character that was developed. How did they do that?'"

Slowly, as she discusses Malcolm, the television link-
age segues to a discussion of character development that
is not specific to text or TV. "You know, he is very intel-
ligent for his age and because of that he is an outcast,"
she says of Malcolm. Once the students understand the

core concept of character development, she then quietly shifts gears and discusses the traits of a character in the book they were reading so her students can understand how to express character development in the written word. It's not teaching to the test—*Malcolm in the Middle* will never appear on the D.C. test. But it's teaching them how to understand character development when it's presented on a D.C. test.

What Tatum does works: the students are engaged and proficiency levels have soared. Near the end of the year, Tatum's students threw a surprise party for her thirty-fourth birthday. Nearly every child and nearly every parent contributed something toward the big event, even if that something was as small as a streamer or some confetti. "Everyone had this intricate part to play in this huge production," she said. "They all came together. It really moved me to the point where I called each parent and through the bubbling of tears told them how grateful I was and every single parent told me how I changed their child's life."

HILLARY HARPER

Harper grew up in Greensboro, North Carolina, went to boarding school in Alexandria, Virginia, right across the Potomac from the District of Columbia, and graduated from the University of North Carolina, where she majored in interpersonal communications studies. Harper, twenty-three, is a first-year teacher out of the D.C. Teaching Fellows program, a program launched by Rhee's New Teacher Project that selects promising teachers, usually not education majors, trains them to be ready for the classroom, and allows them to pursue a teaching credential while working. At the time I interviewed her, Harper was the youngest teacher at Sousa and one of only a handful of white teachers there. "The primary reason I came to D.C. was Michelle Rhee," she said. "I read a lot of education policy and my master's is in educational public policy. I was amazed by what Rhee was doing. I am very data-driven, another reason I agree with Michelle Rhee. The data doesn't lie." Most impressive to Harper was the salary incentive program Rhee was trying to get off the ground, where the highest-performing teachers would be paid like bankers. "I liked the idea of teaching being as valued as any other profession."

Harper chose not just D.C. but also Anacostia. "I knew I wanted to be challenged and I wanted to fix the achievement gap," she said. "In D.C. it's like a tale of two cities. As soon as you cross the Anacostia River, D.C. turns from green to brown." Among Anacostia schools, she found just the principal she was looking for in Jordon. "He has a very clear goal on student achievement and isn't going to let anything get in the way. He calls them smoke clouds—teacher drama, anything that isn't there for the sole purpose of student achievement."

All that sounds inspirational, but as any newbie teacher in a tough school will tell you—including Michelle Rhee from her Baltimore experience—idealism isn't enough once the first bell rings. In Harper's case, her first bell rang on a special education class that included eleven boys and one girl. "It was a disaster. They saw me and walked all over me." But Harper refused to back down. While she struggled with classroom management, she figured out a way to teach through the noise. "I think the big thing was getting student buy-in, letting them know what they were working for and letting them know I care. They know that even if they make me mad the day before, even if they absolutely killed me and ran over me the day before, I'm going to smile and greet everyone as they come in the door. They don't want to let me down. They realize that I am there for them when they might not have lots of stability at home."

Watching Harper work a classroom shows she has learned something from those early disastrous days. Her voice breaking with hoarseness, her blond hair spilling out from her bun, Harper is relentless as she circles the room playing cheerleader to small groups of students working on prealgebra problems. "Don't give up on me, Douglas!" Part of her strategy is organizing competitions, which is especially popular with boys. Each table is a team and for sitting quietly, getting answers right, working well together they get points, which accumulate toward extra credit toward their grades, maybe candy or pizza.

Whatever Harper is doing at Sousa, it's working. In just one year she boosted the percentage of her students scoring proficient in math from 47 to 78. "She also had 17 percent of her students scoring at the advance level and only four students scoring below basic," said LaKeisha Wells, Sousa's assistant principal for intervention. That kind of intensity takes a toll and not just on her voice. But Harper plans to teach at Sousa for another three years. After that, she hopes to find a policy job that focuses on reducing urban achievement gaps.

COURTNEY ALDRIDGE

Aldridge, thirty, is a D.C. girl raised by parents who carefully sidestepped D.C. schools. Her father, who has a law degree, worked for the D.C. government. For Aldridge, home was northwest D.C. and education was a series of demanding Catholic schools and then LaSalle University in Philadelphia. When it came time to teach, she wanted to return to the District, and not necessarily the more comfortable northwest neighborhoods. "I've worked in recreation centers and every time I came to this neighborhood it disturbed me," she said of Anacostia. "It seemed like they were being ignored because of their circumstances."

Although Aldridge's teaching career began in neighboring Prince George's County, after Rhee arrived she applied to teach in D.C. schools. "Being from here, I wanted to be part of the change. I knew this school would be a challenge, a lot of work, but I wanted to see if I could succeed," said Aldridge, who teaches sixth-grade math. "Some kids think they can come in here and because they don't have anything, a piece of paper and a pencil, that they are not going to learn. No, I am going to give you that pencil. I'm going to give you paper and now let's get started. That was half the battle, for them, to recognize that I wasn't just going to accept them not having anything."

Aldridge has a noisy, high-energy teaching style—lots of jokes thrown in. Very different from Tatum's quiet class or Harper's class, where lots of learning games are played. Different styles, but similar results: in her first year at Sousa, Aldridge took her homeroom class from 30 percent proficient to 83 percent. Unheard of, especially in Anacostia.

How did these kids ever hit those academic depths? "Before Mr. Jordon came in, the kids were allowed to do what they wanted," Aldridge said. "The staff would say, 'Oh, these kids are from Southeast,' or 'They're just unruly or intolerable so they can't learn.' . . . What you have to do is kind of polish them down, shine them up, and say to them: 'Wait a minute, you don't have to act like that.'"

Aldridge acknowledges that D.C. has been afflicted with too many teachers who believed they were hamstrung by the kids they taught. Most of the teachers now at Sousa have snap, said Aldridge, the belief that students can overcome circumstances to meet academic goals. "You can tell a teacher who is willing to go up and beyond," she said. "They're the ones who are always around, even when they're not getting paid to do something. I'm thirty and I'm tired. I get up at 5:15 a.m. and get here by 7 a.m. When I leave here, I am exhausted."

Life Beyond Sousa

The dramatic changes taking place at Sousa have just begun to sink in with parents, says Pittman, the dean of students. "They notice the difference because of siblings who went there before. Now, they want to add a ninth grade so the kids don't have to leave." Most would credit the changes to Dwan Jordon's arrival. Michelle Rhee was more an elusive figure, akin to a general manager who hired a good coach. Part of the resentment against Rhee in some parts of D.C. appears rooted in the fact that it took a Korean American to actually improve schools— after a long string of black schools chiefs produced no improvements. It's been tough for some to come to terms with that fact, but not for Pittman, who is African American. "When something is not working, you don't look at color anymore," he says. "She's the lady who came to town [and succeeded], has kids in the schools, and that's what it's about."

The pride the neighborhood takes in the school is apparent. Despite the local goings on after dark, the sparkling Sousa grounds (the school recently underwent a complete renovation) remain unmarred. Not a spot of graffiti. Pittman points to the young men hanging out at midday. "A lot of guys love this school and will protect this school," he said. "They don't allow graffiti, they won't let dogs on the grass, they don't drink over here or throw bottles on the ground because their siblings go to the school. I don't have a problem with these guys."

During the day—never at night—Pittman, who lives in northwest Washington, D.C., visits students' homes regularly, usually to check on attendance problems, and never experiences problems. Often, he removes his suit jacket, just to make sure he doesn't resemble a landlord with an eviction notice. The reception is always good, including from older siblings. "They'll make sure their brother and sisters get an education."

· · · · ·

Until the recent improvements, parents had two choices when their children left Sousa after eighth grade: Anacostia High School, which was both out of control and academically deficient until Rhee assigned a charter operator to take over, or a charter high school, Friendship Collegiate Academy, a mile north of Sousa, in the opposite direction of Anacostia. Parents view Friendship as a school with good discipline and respectable academics. The big plus for them, however, is the trip to school. To reach Friendship, they walk through a business district. Lots of security, lots of watching eyes. To reach Anacostia, they walk through sketchy neighborhoods, past boarded-up apartment buildings that draw a rough crowd.

These days, however, with the surge in test scores and boost in reputation, Sousa is starting to place more students across the river in public high schools that only accept transfer requests from better students. "They saw the kids' test scores and how they interact and said it would be a pleasure to have them," said Pittman. To let parents know about those better options across the river—only a couple of miles away but a place many Anacostia parents and students have never seen—Sousa staff members arranged for the more elite, invitation-only public schools, such as Banneker and School Without Walls, to come to Anacostia and recruit. They provided buses to take students and parents to visit other D.C. high schools and see those neighborhoods. "Last year we had a student accepted to Duke Ellington, the performing arts high school located in an upscale Georgetown neighborhood, and the mother was like, 'Where is it? How will I get there to see it?'" She had never been there—a distance of only six or seven miles.

· · · · ·

Jordon's focus is absolute. His professional life remains in the classroom and the hallways and he blocks out all outside distractions, including writers. On more than one occasion I was left waiting in an empty room for a promised interview. Once, I convinced a security guard to escort me to teachers' classrooms when Jordon wasn't there to do it. It wasn't rudeness; to Jordon, I was just a distraction, a "smoke cloud." I had nothing to do with teaching and learning, so why bother?

Midway through the reporting on Sousa, I pressed Jordon on the teachers he had fired. He demurred. He just didn't want to think anymore about ineffective teachers whose removal had already consumed a year of his valuable time.

THE FLIP SIDE: JOHNSON MIDDLE SCHOOL

Is Sousa an outlier, the result of an unusually talented and inspired principal and therefore not likely to be duplicated? Although Sousa is not Rhee's only successful middle school, it is the only one in Anacostia. For contrast, consider Johnson Middle School, a short drive away. The two schools have student populations similar in demographics, similar neighborhood conditions—but vastly different student outcomes. The principal Rhee tapped to turn around Johnson was David Markus, a white man with a trace of a Boston accent, sixteen years of successful teaching, a master's from Harvard, and experience leading civil rights tours of the South. Trained through the highly regarded New Leaders for New Schools program, he had been a successful assistant principal at D.C.'s Cardozo High School.

With some principals, Rhee would take a deep breath, cross her fingers, and hope for the best. Markus wasn't like that; she had a good feeling about this appointment. Markus told Rhee he was up for a challenge, especially at the middle school level. As a high school assistant principal he saw far too many students who had been cheated out of adequate academic preparation in middle school, which greatly reduced their odds of making it to graduation. Send me to a tough middle school, he told Rhee. And Rhee delivered that challenge: Johnson Middle School.

That was in 2009. More than a year later, in June 2010, I arrived at Johnson just moments after Markus learned he had not been asked to return the next year. The staff hadn't yet been informed—that would come at a 3:15 p.m. meeting. Despite the awkward circumstances, Markus graciously gave me a tour of the building and discussed Johnson, a school where, after his year as principal, only 12 percent of the students were proficient in reading, 15 percent in math—roughly the same student outcome as when he took over. (The year before Jordon took over Sousa, 16 percent of the students were proficient in reading, 14 percent in math. In 2010, those numbers had climbed to 41 and 46 percent, respectively.)

"When I arrived, this building was a mess on so many levels," said Markus. "The building was dilapidated and falling apart. Right before I came, the entire front office was excessed." He had no business manager, an assistant principal for intervention who came from an affluent suburb, and many teachers on ninety-day plans, a midway step toward removal. Johnson's reputation was so bad that few teachers wanted jobs there; the school traditionally relied on hiring in September from the pool of teachers who had been fired from other schools but still guaranteed jobs under the union contract.

Then, things worsened. A week before the faculty were due to arrive, Markus suffered a heart attack. "They put a stent in and I was back a week later for the first day of school," he said. "But I missed that key week, when you introduce yourself to the faculty and set the tone for the year."

A tour of the building confirmed his observations about the school. There were unpleasant odors throughout the building. Most, apparently, arose from mold in the ceiling, a result of years of leakage from HVAC pipes that only occasionally work. Many of the windows were so smeared that the outside world was barely visible, the result of repeated paint-ball attacks by neighborhood kids. There was no library, just a "resource" room used by volunteer tutors where the odor was particularly overpowering. One upstairs room remained locked and empty—it had been trashed by out-of-control students who walked all over an industrial arts teacher. Desks had been pitted with classroom-supplied screwdrivers and hammers and the walls were smeared with graffiti using classroom-supplied paint. A boy's bathroom had three toilets but no stalls, no toilet paper, no soap, no towels. Johnson is scheduled for a modernization, Markus said, but the repair plans had to be peeled back due to budget cuts. Schools like this, argued Markus, are a three-year project. One-year turn-arounds are just not realistic.

· · · · ·

If Markus is right, then Rhee was being not just overly expectant and harsh but also hurting D.C. schools by churning through principals and failing to nurture positive change. It's true that Rhee's record of prodigious firings make suburban, and even many urban, superintendents cringe. Churn, they say, only resets the clock to zero. But Rhee was as confident in firing Markus as she was in hiring him. Dwan Jordan, she says, could have legitimately said some of the same things about Sousa when he entered the building—Sousa was a dumping ground for bad teachers with terrible test scores. Johnson Middle School has fewer than three hundred students, Rhee pointed out. A typical urban middle school has closer to seven hundred. "How could [Markus] have done it? With as few as three hundred kids it is absolutely possible to create change." Nor was Rhee sympathetic about the paintball-smeared windows: "Do you not manage your custodians? Can you not get them to clean?"

The bottom line: Markus broke Rhee's basic rule when he failed to seize control of the building in the first year. "I visited the school several times," she said. "I watched him. I don't know that I would have been able to pick this up in a hiring interview but he is just not the kind of guy who commands respect among kids. When I was talking with him kids would run by him, yell over him, and throw things. When a principal commands respect, they may be running but when they see the principal they stop. That's basic. Basic!"

Who's right here? Based on my observations, Rhee. At one point Markus took me into a classroom to introduce me to one of his teachers. There were only four girls in the room and they had been given end-of-year privileges to play computer games. While we were talking, the girls launched into a high-decibel yelling match. Both Markus and the teacher struggled to restore order even while pleading for respect because "there's a visitor in the room." Whatever that secret sauce is that some principals have to command respect everywhere in the school building, Markus didn't have it that day. And although it's true that he was saddled with an awful building and Jordon had been dealt a newly refurbished one, that can't be the only explanation. Another Anacostia middle school had just been renovated and the test scores there lagged well behind Sousa. That principal was also fired.

· · · · ·

Only about half the original principals in place when Rhee arrived are still working for D.C. schools. Rhee says that outside superintendents are aghast at her turnover rate and have no idea of the realities she faced. "When you're in the situation we're in, the dire straits, you have to know when to cut bait." She might be able to have patience developing a principal for a couple years when three-quarters of the students are proficient. "But when you're talking about a school in which 10 percent of the students are proficient and kids are running around . . . show me a superintendent anywhere who in that circumstance feels comfortable looking a parent in the eye saying, 'We believe that with two more years of professional development that David Markus would be good.'"

What's telling about the tale of the two Anacostia schools is the reaction from Rhee's critics. After the 2009–2010 school year ended, *The Washington Post* ran a feature story on the gains made at Sousa.[7] The article was generally positive but quoted one of the fired teachers anonymously: "If a teacher is sincere, I don't think everything needs to be stacked on the test scores," said the teacher, who spoke on the condition of anonymity because she wants to teach elsewhere. "Also, it depends on the children you get."

It was the Slowe sign all over: we're doing the best we can with the flawed children sent our way. That message, however, was embraced by Rhee's fiercest critics, even about the successes at Sousa. At the Web site The Washington Teacher,[8] which regularly vilified Rhee, the headline for an essay commenting on the *Post* article was: "The Tyranny of DC's Sousa Middle School Principal Dwan Jordon." The piece by Candi Peterson, who wrote the blog and later in 2010 won the job of vice president of the Washington Teachers Union (thereby offering an insight into the thinking of current union leadership), ignored the fact that test scores improved because Jordon forced out ineffective teachers. Instead, it focused on the grievances filed by the teachers pushed out. Wrote one teacher, referring to the improve-or-lose-your-job ninety-day plan: "It was very common for most teachers on the ninety-day plan to be observed at least three times a day, yes three times a day." In truth, multiple observances of teachers failing to teach are what should be happening in all failing schools.

Ironically, the obvious story arising from the tale of the two Anacostia middle schools was ignored by both the *Post* and the union critics: was firing most of the pre-Rhee teachers a requirement for making dramatic progress? It's hard to draw any other conclusion. It appears that broad and lasting student gains were possible in D.C. schools only if two-thirds of the teachers who were there when Rhee arrived got pushed out and replaced by far better teachers. And what played out at Sousa would have been only the beginning for D.C.'s schools had Rhee remained at the helm.

Chapter Eight

Up from the Foundations: The Challenge of High School Reform

George W. Bush's signature education law, No Child Left Behind, which he regards as his greatest domestic achievement, had a fatal flaw conveniently timed to float to the surface after Bush finished his second term. Nobody— not the U.S. Department of Education, not states, not superintendents, not principals—had even the slightest clue as to what to do about the schools that kept missing test-score targets, known under the law as *adequate yearly progress,* or AYP. After five years of failure, schools were supposed to go into "restructuring" to turn themselves around.[1] Yet nobody had a proved tool kit to achieve those turnarounds.

Oops.

Turning around an elementary school is extremely challenging; a middle school, next to impossible. High schools fit into the "beyond impossible" category. Even the high-flying charter management organizations, groups such as KIPP and Uncommon Schools, stay away from parachuting into troubled high schools. They prefer to build their own schools from scratch and few go past eighth grade. Attempts to turn around awful urban high schools are so rare that they are apt to draw the attention of multitudes of politicians, other reformers, and national journalists. Just look at the Green Dot Public Schools charter group's takeover of Locke High School in Los Angeles, which overnight became the topic of many newspaper and magazine pieces. A failing inner-city high school is a morass of issues: race, poverty, gangs, teen pregnancy, and a hopeless job market in the immediate neighborhood. It is the tip of the pyramid of failed elementary and middle schools that sets the stage for future dropouts before students ever set foot in the high school. Transform an urban high school that long ago sunk into despair? Who would even try such craziness?

Michelle Rhee. When Rhee arrived in Washington she discovered that under No Child Left Behind, twenty-seven of the city's schools faced restructuring—including *all ten* high schools.[2] To translate what that means: in 2007 only 5 percent of the students at Ballou High School were proficient in reading, 6 percent in math. At Anacostia High School, the proficiency rates were 8 percent and 6 percent.

· · · · ·

Many in the district, especially at the school level, seemed unaware of the mandate to reconstitute. "The school district hadn't talked to the schools to tell them they were going to have to restructure," Rhee said. "Most of the people I talked to were like, 'What is restructuring? What is AYP?' . . . It should have been the district's responsibility to communicate with the schools and parents: here is what is going to happen if we don't meet this year's or next year's goal." Restructuring was laid out in federal law and a long time in coming. But instead it looked like an unwelcome surprise—courtesy of Michelle Rhee and her broom.

But what to do about it? Before Rhee, superintendents' MO was to write a restructuring plan and then do nothing about it. It was easy to get away with. The Bush administration certainly had no plans to step in and crack the whip. NCLB may have been a federal law, but the feds knew better to jump into this tar pit. Failing schools were D.C.'s problems to solve. Rhee opted to do what previous D.C. superintendents had chosen not to do: she forced at least some of the schools to face their failures and enter *real* restructuring.

The schools, of course, were not happy. "When I started meeting with school groups I realized, first of all, they were in shock," Rhee says. "Second, they were indignant. And third, they wanted to just create their own restructuring plan. I was like, 'If you had the ability to create a plan that would turn this school around, I'm assuming you would have done that in the last five years.'"

Rhee's options were limited. In other urban school districts, a state takeover is always an option (rarely attempted and almost never successful, but at least it is an option). D.C. had no state to execute a takeover. Rhee could have chosen the same path embraced by multiple urban school chiefs at that time: breaking large high schools into smaller, more intimate schools, an approach championed by the Gates Foundation, perhaps the most major player in education reform. "Michelle said, 'No, that's not what we're going to do,'" said Justin Cohen, a school turnaround specialist whom Rhee tapped to come up with solutions for the high schools. "Smallness or bigness wasn't what was making high schools fail. It was the quality of instruction and quality of the management and infrastructure."

Rhee didn't have the resources to take on all the failing D.C. high schools at once, so she searched the country for high school takeover specialists willing to do the job—"partners" who would take control of a school while keeping governance within DCPS. She chose two partners to take over three high schools. This is the story of one of those schools: Dunbar High School.

Taking on Dunbar

While every regular high school in Washington faced restructuring in 2007, the biggest embarrassment from a historical perspective had to be Dunbar High School. The school, located in Ward 5, a ten-minute walk from the city's much-touted new convention center, was once known as Preparatory High School for Colored Youth. In 1916 the school was renamed in honor of poet Paul Laurence Dunbar. During Jim Crow years and beyond, Dunbar was an academic mecca for black Americans, something of a college disguised as a high school where black intellectuals with advanced degrees came to teach because they couldn't land jobs at universities. Many families moved to Washington just to send their children to Dunbar. The school turned out a Who's Who of black twentieth-century intellectuals, such as Benjamin O. Davis Sr., who became the first black Army general, and Charles R. Drew, a pioneer in blood transfusions who helped develop large-scale blood banks at the beginning of World War II. Dunbar is also the alma mater of D.C. Mayor Vincent Gray, the council chairman who successfully challenged Adrian Fenty for mayor in 2010.

But over time neighborhoods change. As housing projects arose in the neighborhoods around Dunbar, much of the black middle class moved to neighboring Prince George's County in Maryland, and academically aggressive charter schools siphoned off the better students who stayed in D.C. In an astonishingly short period of time, Dunbar High School went from being the pride of black America to what Rhee found in 2007, a local and national shame. On my first visit to Dunbar, my African-born cab driver took one look at the building and muttered, "This is a high school? Looks like a prison."

It didn't take long for Rhee to determine that Dunbar, attended by 750 students, needed a complete reconstitution, which meant that the staff had to reapply for their jobs and an outside operator was chosen to take over. After a quick "speed dating" game in which Rhee and community members reviewed the few takeover candidates on the national scene, they arrived at Friends of Bedford, a charismatic band of ambitious educators who launched the hugely successful Bedford Academy High School in New York City and then concluded they had the chops to expand their brand.[3] Dunbar would be their first attempt.

The key operator at Bedford was George Leonard, a suave, intense man with a preternaturally soothing voice, a sharp sense of humor, a near-perfect ability to lock eyeballs, and that indefinable, impossible-to-find ability to reason with unruly students. Better yet, he had the ability to mentor talented deputy administrators so they could learn to do the same. Maybe not on Leonard's level but close enough.

· · · · ·

Few forget their first contact with George Leonard. Justin Cohen, who was in charge of the process of selecting a partner for Dunbar, prefers to act out his memory of his first meeting. I met him at the Corner Bakery in Washington's Union Station. As Cohen tells the story, it all started with a meeting he set up in D.C. so that Rhee's staff could meet Leonard and his assistants. "Leonard proceeds, in his George Leonard way, to lean in and tell me about how great Bedford Academy High School is," Cohen says. This is indisputably true; the high school they launched in a gritty Brooklyn neighborhood is a great school by any standards. At that time it was graduating 100 percent of its kids and nearly all were going on to four-year colleges.

At this point, Cohen, continuing the re-creation and, pretending to be Leonard, reaches down and pulls a fresh piece of paper from his briefcase, placing it on the table before me. Leaning in and locking eyeballs, he loudly crushes the paper—an act meant to symbolize the total collapse of student discipline Leonard had witnessed in D.C. schools. "Kids in DCPS are not paying attention!" (At this point in the re-creation, other diners are looking over to check out the excitement.) Leonard then launched into a fast-paced lecture about the chaos in D.C. schools. "He's banging on the table, telling everyone how terrible this school is and how great Bedford Academy is and everyone is sitting around nodding," Cohen says. "I'm agreeing with him. Finally, I said, 'George, it was a pleasure meeting you and your team, and I can see your model is good and how well your leadership team has gelled, but how that does help us in D.C.?'"

At that point, he says Leonard dramatically (and unexpectedly) offered to move his entire leadership team to Washington. Friends of Bedford, he said, had already developed a succession plan for its New York school and was ready to expand. Cohen says, "I was like, 'Now you are speaking my language, now we're talking about something compelling.'"

Soon after that Cohen went to New York to visit Bedford Academy, expecting to see what we think of as the typical model for a high-achieving urban school: students in uniform, standing in lines, rigidly disciplined. "Bedford was not that," Cohen says. "Kids were in clothes they wanted to wear. But it wasn't an undisciplined culture. You couldn't swear in that school or chew gum or be disrespectful. But you could wear your clothes and be a kid in the hallway every now and then. When it came to the rules, everyone knew what they were. It defied the conventional wisdom of what an urban high school had to be." Cohen called Rhee and told her she had to see the school, which she did a few weeks later. Rhee was impressed by Bedford Academy but uneasy with Leonard's style. "George is a little blustery for me. My style and what I always to instill in my folks is that we will underpromise and overdeliver. George had the potential to overpromise and underdeliver, which is not what you want." Still, Bedford's success in New York was undeniable and the alternatives for Dunbar were few. It wasn't long before Leonard and his team were handed the keys to Dunbar.[4]

THE BEDFORD TAKEOVER

Despite his success at building a successful school in one of New York's most challenging neighborhoods, Leonard wasn't prepared for what he would find at Dunbar. During

the 2008–2009 school year, Leonard and his team were supposed to observe how Dunbar operated so they could prepare to fully take over the high school the following year.
The "planning year" didn't quite work out that way. When
I met Leonard in early spring 2010, I asked him to lead me
on a school tour and describe what he found when he had
arrived two years earlier. Pausing in the library, he looked out
a window and pointed to the athletic field below. "The students used to go to the track field for lunch," he said. "The
entire student body was in the bleachers. They were smoking reefer, climbing fences, exchanging drugs with the community. It was a horrible scene that was devoid of any type
of supervision." Worst were the hallways, which at Dunbar
wrap around internal, open ramps that connect the floors.
"The first class change I saw, they weren't moving. You didn't
see any motion. And they were vulgar. When you looked at
them they would stare back with that, 'Who are you staring
at? Do you have a problem?' We were first known as the FBI,
because we always had suits on."

Dunbar's open classroom design added to the chaos.
Not only was the noise deafening, but classrooms also became
open to marauders, some of whom weren't even students.
Doors were left open for teenagers to come and go as they
pleased, whether or not they were authorized to be in the
building. They would sweep into a class, grab a necklace or
bracelet off a girl, and disappear—all amidst what was passing for teaching and learning. One teacher got hit by a cup of
urine thrown by a student on an upper-level ramp and fights
were common. "Even though we were supposed to just be
observing that first year, we had to become more proactive
because of the dangers in the building," Leonard said. The

Friends of Bedford team sought and received permission from Rhee to make some security changes.

The next school year, when the time came for Leonard and his team to formally take over, a lot more changed. Almost overnight, and just moments before the students arrived, classroom dividers went up that ended the open classroom insanity. The filthy, moldy carpet that covered the notorious ramp was removed. The nonfunctional computers in the library were repaired. Dress codes were imposed and the security became airtight. Students were confined to the lunchroom during lunch.

Leonard and his team, still dressed in their serious suits, were everywhere and were unhesitant about going nose-to-nose with students. He explained, "It was, 'Go to class. Pull up your pants. Take your hands off her. No, it's not okay to say that to her. Why are you on her? Why is she on you? What did you say about your mother? What did he say about his mother? Take that hat off. Too much jewelry. Too much gold in your mouth. Where do you belong? Are you even a student here?' It was like that for a year."

· · · · ·

The saddest part of the takeover might have been when the Friends of Bedford team unearthed the student academic transcripts or what passed as transcripts. The incompetence in the counseling department was so pervasive that many students were forced to spend far longer in high school than necessary, simply because their counselors had never lined up the correct courses for them to graduate. When Leonard asked the counselors how that could have happened, the answer was always, "I did the best I could." When pressed further, the staff members responsible for the debacle would eventually start blaming the kids, the parents, and the neighborhood conditions. "It's a sad commentary because a lot of these folks who worked here come from these neighborhoods and were able to rise above," he said. Leonard and his new administrators fired nearly all the counselors and began rebuilding the student transcripts.[5]

· · · · ·

The strangest challenge for the Bedford team was one they had never predicted: athletics. They weren't surprised that many of the students, especially the guys, valued sports over academics. Especially in urban high schools, dreaming of making it in the NFL or NBA is a common fantasy. What the Bedford team hadn't anticipated was how many parents, teachers, principals, and politicians went along with the sports-over-academics emphasis. In some cases, students with D averages, or even mostly Fs, were allowed to play football. Students assigned to mandatory tutoring were allowed to pursue football first, tutoring second, if at all. Coaches had complete autonomy over their programs.

Once in a long while, a D.C. student has made the pros—and that sliver of success appeared to shape attitudes. "There's like, what, fifty players on the football team, and over the past four years you've had two make it to the NFL," said Nakia Gaston, chief operating officer for Bedford. "What about the others?" Immediately, the Bedford team imposed academic standards on players and enforced tutoring rules. That didn't go over well; some coaches left for other jobs.[6] "You know, we disturbed the peace," said Gaston. "We're here to make necessary changes. We never shy away from academics being the priority for us, so anyone not on that same agenda will not be happy. . . . We were not popular because this is an athletic town, bottom-line."

The unhealthy mix in D.C. between academics and athletics is hard to hide. In June 2010, a *Washington Post* sportswriter exposed the problems D.C. high school athletes have meeting college academic standards. Their high school GPAs might look good but there was no real learning behind those diplomas.

> In nearly three dozen interviews, athletes, parents, coaches, guidance counselors, and school administrators identified four primary areas of concern that they said are hurting student-athletes in the D.C. public school system who aspire to play their sport in college: outdated graduation requirements; inadequate standardized-test preparation; a lack of understanding of NCAA requirements by guidance counselors; and loopholes in athletic eligibility standards that allow students to stay eligible for sports but ultimately come up short of NCAA standards.[7]

Rhee was not surprised. "A huge percentage of our high schools kids are not enrolling in the appropriate classes that are going to prepare them for college," she said. So a D.C. graduate who enters college typically must take noncredit remedial classes. Rhee hired a new athletic director for the district and told him, "A lot of coaches in DCPS want to win, and they want to have the championship jackets and all that, but they are not promoting scholarships, they aren't promoting the kids being scholar-athletes." The emphasis, she said, had to change.

. . . . .

By the 2010 school year, the Dunbar hallways were mostly under control and many new teachers headed up classrooms. Less than half the prereconstitution teachers remained. Any experienced educator could walk through the hallways and observe at least a moderate amount of teaching and learning taking place. Baby steps, perhaps, but considering the chaos that had ruled Dunbar, this was a revolution. "We want to bring the school to a point where the students are taking more advanced placement classes and this is more of a college preparatory high school," said Leonard. "Everybody needs an option to go to college whether or not they choose to or not. But you have to have the option."

The students I interviewed during my visits to Dunbar gave me a pretty uniform story. Before Friends of Bedford took over, the place was wild. Depending on the temperament of the student being interviewed—you have to give them points for honesty—this was either a good thing or a bad thing.

Before the changes, "I kind of liked the fact that we had freedom," said Ebony Bennett, a senior. "I was introduced to things I wouldn't normally see. You had to grow up fast. You could stand out in the hallway or go into class. No one made you do anything you didn't want to do; we made up our own set of rules. It was kind of fun." As a cheerleader, she ran with the in-crowd, which afforded her some protection. Although she conceded that Dunbar had been hectic prior to the Rhee takeover, she said she never felt unsafe.

Donald Williams, a tenth-grader, was less enthusiastic about the pre-Rhee Dunbar. "There were fights like every week. . . . It was kind of like a zoo." Demetria Wilson, another tenth-grader, agreed: "When I first came into the building, it was just loud, like everybody was out of place. People didn't know where they were supposed to be. There were people just standing in the hallways, socializing. Some kids were smoking in the staircase. . . . My ninth-grade year, girls pulled out knives. It was crazy."

As for academics, the students could come up with only one teacher, a beloved longtime biology teacher, who somehow managed to maintain academic standards. Rescuing a school like Dunbar involves far more than just seizing control of the hallways—something Friends of Bedford succeeded in doing, based on my visits and student descriptions. But in a building where students could name just one effective teacher, a full academic recovery remains a distant goal. Leonard and his team, however, seemed to be headed in the right direction: in their first year there, the number of students testing proficient or advanced in reading went from 18 to 32 percent.

2010–2011: The Success Unravels

At the end of the 2009–2010 school year, Leonard fired the principal there, Stephen Jackson, for "undermining" Bedford's efforts.[8] Efforts to name a new principal, however, sputtered and eventually Leonard stepped into that role. What happened next is in dispute, but DCPS administrators say class schedules weren't prepared in time, which triggered early chaos from which the high school never recovered. Interim Chancellor Kaya Henderson, appointed after Rhee left, visited Dunbar unannounced in late November 2010 and found large groups of students hanging out in front of the school. "The line at the metal detector looked like the airport at Thanksgiving. I walked around the building and found three classrooms where there were students, but no adults. I asked the students and they said, 'Oh, you know, teachers sometimes don't come. We're all right.' That was a significant problem for me. In other classrooms teachers were there but there was no learning going on." That visit, combined with a meeting with teachers, sealed the fate of Friends of Bedford. On December 9, Henderson removed Friends of Bedford and returned Jackson as principal.[9] Supporters of Friends of Bedford charged that Henderson caved to political pressure from Mayor-Elect Gray who wanted to disassemble many of Rhee's reforms. The reality is that the change at Dunbar was sealed with Henderson's visit.

In the end, the lesson relearned is the "oops" loophole in No Child Left Behind. Nobody has a sure-fire plan for saving failing schools, especially high schools, and especially high schools like Dunbar. Although Henderson would never say this, DCPS essentially had no choice but to abandon its teaching-and-learning goals at Dunbar for the rest of the school year. It was back to the first-year basic goal for any troubled school: lock down the school and regain control.

Chapter Nine

RHEE'S CRITICS FIND A
WINNING STORYLINE

Many social revolutions reach a turning point when the forces of resistance successfully redefine change in ways favorable to them. At that point, the revolution may still seem alive and unstoppable but in truth it has been steered into a dead end. And so it was with Michelle Rhee's push to breathe academic life into the D.C. public schools. In her case, that turning point happened at the most unlikely of places, a reasonably functional school located in one of D.C.'s nicest neighborhoods: Hardy Middle School. The trigger for the turning point was more predictable: race politics.

THE HARDY BACKLASH

Many parents who send their children to Hardy, located in an upscale white Georgetown neighborhood, would describe it an arts and music magnet school. Except it isn't, really. It's a neighborhood school that an enterprising and popular principal, Patrick Pope, got designated as a school with an arts and music focus. Nobody has to prove proficiency on the clarinet to gain admission. Hardy just seems like a magnet because many middle-class African American families from other parts of the city have used the district's "out of boundary" school choice process to send their children there and they like the arts theme.

Those students make up most of the Hardy population; although the elementary schools in the Hardy feeder pattern are mostly white, in 2010 Hardy was two-thirds black and less than 10 percent white. (Many white families in the area who are comfortable sending their children to public elementary school find other options for middle school and beyond.) For the Hardy black parents, Pope's school has been a blessing. It's a safe public school with a respectable academic record and an arts focus they treasure. On top of everything else, the recently remodeled building looks better than some elite private schools I've visited.

Logic would suggest that Hardy Middle School would be a distant blip on Rhee's radar of reform targets. It wasn't a failing school. Hardy families, the Hardy principal, Hardy teachers, the city councilmembers representing all of those folks—they all seemed to like Hardy just the way it was. In a sea of horribly disgraceful D.C. schools, Hardy pretty much worked. The operative phrase is "pretty much." In 2010, only 57 percent of the black students were proficient in reading, 50 percent in math. By D.C. standards, however, that was pretty close to success. If it ain't broke, why fix it?

Michelle Rhee used to be invited to "living room" sessions throughout the city, where parents would have the chance to discuss with her whatever was on their minds. At one such session with parents who lived in one of the upscale

neighborhoods around Hardy, Rhee got an earful. Why
can't Hardy be a traditional middle school for our kids? That
seemed to her a reasonable request. Few would consider the
parents in these upscale neighborhoods deprived in any way,
but this was the only part of the city that lacked a high school.
Why not find some way to bring more middle-class families
right around Hardy into the school to embrace the school
district they had shunned for decades? That way, maybe one
day in the future, Georgetown could even have its own high
school. Rhee's solution: stop pretending that Hardy was anything other than a regular neighborhood school and hang out
a welcome mat for the immediate neighborhood. At the same
time: build a true, citywide arts and music magnet middle
school and tap Pope to design it.

Assigning Pope to the central office to plan the new
school seemed like a perfect way to achieve multiple goals. To
Rhee and her staff, it looked as if Pope's student selection process at Hardy weeded out lower-income black children who
might not fit in (read: be disruptive) and possibly even special
education students.[1] (Pope takes strong exception to the suggestion that his application process discriminated against any
students.[2]) Tapping a new principal from one of the feeder
elementary schools would send the right signal to the neighborhood and also guarantee that Hardy's out-of-boundary
transfer process would be open to a broader set of African
American parents. A win-win.

Except Hardy turned into a lose-lose before anyone had
time to notice. Rhee and others at the central office say they
heard Pope sign off on the new plan, or at least they thought
they did. Overnight there was an outburst of demonstrations
by Hardy students and parents that appeared to have Pope's

blessing. The opposition storyline: Rhee wants to push out black students to make room for wealthy white students. That storyline proved to be effective. The white parents from the neighborhood who originally expressed interest in giving DCPS schools a try withdrew in silence, unwilling to stand up to race politics. Said Rhee: "I would get e-mails all the time from families, both black and white, that said they knew I was doing the right thing, but they weren't going to stand in front of the firing squad." In the end, Rhee's own reputation hurt her. Because so many people knew she was unlikely to back down when she was sure she was right, they let her take all the bullets.

· · · · ·

Those opposed to the Hardy decision were far less shy. Hardy's school band appeared outside DCPS headquarters (during school hours) to protest the changes and demand Pope's return. Students poured into a council meeting to testify before councilmembers very open to anti-Rhee rhetoric. The students delivered: "The sad part is that many students are beginning to view the chancellor as a real-life Dolores Umbridge," said one seventh-grader quoted in *The Washington Post*, referring to a Harry Potter villain.

Rhee was getting creamed. Some of her national supporters, who prior to this had never heard of Hardy Middle School, were practically begging her to reverse her stand. Everyone from Teach for America founder Wendy Kopp to then-New York City Schools Chancellor Joel Klein were getting calls and e-mails with the same message: tell Michelle to drop it. (Klein's response: The moment Michelle stops stirring up controversies is the moment she should resign.)

Clearly, the Hardy controversy had turned toxic. It was at that moment that Rhee made a call that shaped her fate in D.C.: she dug in. She refused to change her position, even when it became clear to everyone, both D.C. insiders and national education reformers, that her insistence on shaking up this obscure, reasonably functional middle school with a happy staff and students threatened her broader agenda. And that had national implications. At that point Rhee's reforms had emerged as the most important education experiment in the nation. What she was already doing in D.C. was what Education Secretary Arne Duncan was trying to persuade other troubled school districts to adopt. Both locally and nationally, a lot was riding on Rhee maintaining decent relations with D.C. voters. Keeping parents happy meant keeping Fenty in office, which meant keeping Rhee in her job. And yet, when sizing up Hardy Middle School, she chose to wager everything on taking a hard line.

To Rhee, the Hardy decision got filtered through her what's-best-for-kids train of logic. Hardy was hardly the academic standout touted by its parents; the school needed academic improvements. Luring more middle-class families, white and black, into a mostly poor and racially isolated school district was a decision that fell into the no-brainer category. And finally, a selection process that separates out the "wrong" sort of black families, as Rhee and her staff concluded Pope was doing, was just wrong. Change would happen, Rhee decided, regardless of the protests. "In the past, DCPS administrators would just fold if something like [these protests] happened," says Rhee. "If there was enough pressure that they'd just say, 'Oh, you can stay.' And I was like, you must not have been paying attention for the last three years, because that's not how I operate." To appreciate the determination with which Rhee made that statement you have to visualize her saying it: her charm disappeared, her voice lowered and the words "you must not have been paying attention" were spit out in rapid succession. It was the persona she assumed in any what's-best-for-the kids debate. It was the *Time* cover.

· · · · ·

Rhee's kids-first logic, however, assumed that Washington, D.C., voters were living in a postracial world. But as Rhee and Fenty would discover on the day of D.C.'s primary election, September 14, 2010 (and as the black mayors of Newark, Detroit, and other cities were discovering), race was still a factor—a big one. In the midst of a severe recession, there was a conflict inherent in the two things residents wanted: good schools and reliable, city-supplied jobs. When Rhee fired central office workers who were embarrassingly bad at their jobs, she assumed D.C. residents would rejoice about better schools coming their way. Instead, many residents saw friends and neighbors losing jobs in a disrespectful manner. The same divide played out when she fired ineffective teachers. The white side of the city saw a school system being rescued; the black side saw heads of households—people they knew and couldn't imagine being bad teachers—losing their jobs. Hardy Middle School fit neatly into that storyline: there's nothing postracial about the appearance of trying to oust black kids in favor of white kids. And finally, a lot of middle-class black Hardy parents were asking: why can't we have this school?

ALIENATING THE COUNCIL

The D.C. Council had no trouble understanding that Washington, D.C., was far from postracial; their ears were closer to the ground. For them, Hardy was the anti-Rhee slow pitch they had been waiting for. Payback time. Rhee entered the Hardy Middle School controversy in a weak position when it came to public relations, especially with council members. It went back to Rhee's arrival in D.C.: her introduction to Vincent Gray late on the eve of her public announcement and the even more casual and last-minute meeting with the rest of the council the next day. Gray and the council were offended and caught off guard, which meant Rhee never got her honeymoon time.

Although Rhee's nomination won unanimous approval from the council, her confirmation hearings set a challenging tone that would only intensify in the coming months. Rhee is a relentless debater. She'll take on anyone and argue them down to a nub, regardless of how much time it takes. Even Rhee's friends say the trait can drive them crazy. Plus, she is equipped with a camel-like constitution—able to debate for hours without a break for food, water, or bathrooms. And that's what she did during the confirmation hearings—took on all comers for eleven hours without a single bathroom break. Only Gray attempted to compete in the endurance contest, as she remembers it. "I thought, I'm not getting up until that dude gets up." Rhee won that battle and may have impressed councilmembers with her intellect and physical fortitude. But they also took away another message: she saw council relations as a competitive event.

In March 2008, Rhee endured another marathon session before the council over the firing of nonunion central office employees. This time she was even more combative. "I think they sort of got a taste of me during that hearing, that this girl is not going to lay down and take a beating." When Councilmember Marion Barry—who as mayor turned the central office into a textbook case of patronage incompetence—protested that workers should get a chance to improve, Rhee didn't pretend to offer a polite response. "I was like, 'This is not about the adults. This is about the kids. Could some of the adults get better? Maybe, but how long are we going to wait?'" The council handed Rhee firing authority, but not unanimously. This time the vote was 10–3. And Rhee thinks that she won with that margin only because the councilmembers thought that would be her one big reform.

· · · · ·

They would soon discover that Rhee had much more change on her mind. Almost immediately Rhee rolled out the school closings (which they learned from the list leaked to the *Post*). With the school closings—not just the fact that they happened but that they happened without input from the councilmembers—Rhee lost what little goodwill she had left with them. Worse, she chose to close no schools in white, upper-income Ward 3. To her, that was simple logic: the schools there were more than full. But logic and politics are two very different creatures.

The big complaint from the council was that she never consulted the community. That accusation may be valid for most of the rapid reforms Rhee unfolded but with school closings she and her top staffers attended countless community hearings. What the councilmembers really meant, of course, is that Rhee didn't first ask permission from *them*, a move that would have doomed Rhee's campaign to shift expenses away from heating empty classrooms. Regardless, the perception endured. Rhee rarely helped her local case with public comments (in this case regarding whether she was being solicitous enough to private funders) such as "I'm not going to pretend to solicit your advice so you'll feel involved, because that's just fake."[3]

Then came Hardy Middle School. Councilmembers grilled Rhee mercilessly. She recalls: "Vince Gray, in one of these hearings, was saying, 'Just change your mind! Everybody makes mistakes. It's okay! Just change your mind!' And I was saying, I don't have a problem changing my mind when I realize I made a mistake. . . . The issue here is that I actually believe that I'm right."

Rhee's decision to ride out what she saw as a short-term public relations setback to achieve a long-term goal mirrors a similarly unpopular decision to sack the principal at Oyster-Adams Bilingual School, a highly respected and successful school attended by her daughters. In all these decisions, Rhee was backed by her top staffers. "These were both decent schools that functioned just fine," said Abigail Smith, Rhee's chief of school transformation. "Parents were trying to get their kids in, teachers generally happy. Why rock the boat? Because at the end of the day, what you are trying to do is create a system where all schools are great. You have to move the terrible ones to okay and then from okay to better. And the schools that are good have to become great. Her drive to do that creates a ton of negativity and there are people saying it is stupid and you have to pick your battles. But that's not how Michelle rolls."

TRIAL BY *POST*

Rhee was making enemies fast, helped by press coverage in *The Washington Post*'s Metro section, which sucked up every controversy between Rhee and councilmembers and Rhee and union leaders but rarely looked at the less glamorous side of what was happening within schools. That's not the fault of Bill Turque, the seasoned political and government reporter assigned to the Rhee beat. Turque was doing exactly what *Post* editors assigned him to do. "We asked Bill to cover Michelle Rhee like she was a big city mayor," said *Post* managing editor Liz Spayd.[4]

Turque confirms that it was "his charge" to cover Rhee and her reforms from a political angle. In previous years, the beat had been covered by two reporters, but he was the sole reporter on the beat, which meant that back-to-back Rhee political controversies, from contract negotiations to teacher firings, dominated his reporting. "In a perfect world I would have gone deeper into the schools but there was a lot going on."

As a result, in the *Post* Metro section, the Hardy story, for example, became all about student and parent protests, not about whether there was merit in reducing the racial and economic isolation found in most of D.C.'s schools. Rhee's move to lay off 266 teachers for budgetary reasons became all about a magazine interview in which it sounded like she was suggesting that some of the fired teachers were hitters or sex offenders. The question of how many of those teachers were low performers no parent would want in front of their child's class went unanswered. The *Post* offered saturation coverage of all Rhee controversies involving the adult players in D.C. schools, which is exactly the directive Turque was handed. The obvious downside of that approach is the *Post*, at least from my perspective, published almost nothing in the school year leading up to the election that might explain why poor kids in D.C. were so far behind similar children in other cities.[5]

The tension between the Metro section and editorial page writer Jo-Ann Armao, who steadfastly supported Rhee at times spilled into public view. At one point during the issue over the magazine quote about abusive teachers, Rhee, who often avoided Turque or tried to deal with him through e-mail, called Armao to give her side of the story. Turque then posted this on his blog:

> The chancellor is clearly more comfortable speaking with Jo-Ann, which is wholly unsurprising. I'm a beat reporter charged with covering, as fully and fairly as I can, an often turbulent story about the chancellor's attempts to fix the District's public schools. The job involves chronicling messy and contentious debates based in both politics and policy, and sometimes publishing information she would rather not see in the public domain.[6] Jo-Ann, on the other hand, sits on an editorial board whose support for the chancellor has been steadfast, protective and, at times, adoring.

Soon after it was posted, the original posting was taken down and modified to remove the "protective" and "adoring" comments.[7] Actually Turque was right. Although the editorial page merited praise for getting the facts of Rhee's reforms correct, its tone had been too partisan. But the Metro section coverage swung too far in the opposite direction. This was the *Post*'s notion of balance?

· · · · ·

On a few occasions, the reporting was more than just puzzling. In July 2010, only two months before the mayoral primary, the *Post*'s story on new test scores for D.C. students cited a drop in elementary school scores as a "setback" for Rhee's reforms. Washington, D.C., is pretty close to a one-news-source town, so the story established this "setback" as the final word on Rhee's reforms, in both print and TV outlets, as voters went to the polls. I heard that message when interviewing voters emerging from the primary polls: Rhee's not that great; test scores just took a dip.

True, elementary scores did dip (although secondary school scores rose). But was that a setback for Rhee's reforms? A simple check of the test scores for the charter school students in Washington, D.C.—students over whom Rhee had no control and who attend a variety of very different schools—reveals strikingly similar "setbacks," often matching up grade by grade, subject by subject. For example, reading scores for sixth-grade DCPS students fell by 10.6 percent. For charter students, they fell by 11 percent. Coincidence? Not likely.

Any explanation other than changes in the test itself would not seem plausible—sixth-graders across the district attending scores of different schools somehow getting the identical literacy "dumbs" on that particular test day? In short, this could not be interpreted as a setback for Rhee's reforms. As this book went to press, the *Post* still had not issued a correction or clarification on that story. The response from the *Post*'s Spayd after I sent her the test data: "There are lots of possible reasons why test scores may have dropped. Yours is one thesis." Turque says that because Rhee staked out test scores as proof of her effectiveness his reporting was fair. "She lives and dies by her data."

· · · · ·

The *Post*'s local columnists, some of whom specialize in writing about black D.C., only added to the circus-like atmosphere surrounding Rhee. Colbert King repeatedly claimed that any improvements in D.C. schools could be traced to Rhee's predecessor, Clifford Janey. And he wasn't the only *Post* columnist or reporter to make that claim, a message that resonated in Washington, D.C.[8] You could catch at cab at Union Station, ask about Michelle Rhee, and hear that she was merely riding Janey's coattails. In Washington, D.C., demonstrating that poor, black children in D.C. didn't have to score at worst-in-the-nation levels was a feat more likely to draw applause for an African American black schools chief than a relatively young Korean American woman.

The sometimes-painful truth is that a long series of African American school superintendents preceding her never produced the positive results achieved under Rhee. That was a bitter message, too bitter for many to swallow. Hence, the Janey theory. Janey is not only a nice guy (I knew him a little when we were both in Rochester, New York) but a thoroughly competent schools administrator who, after leaving D.C., took over the schools in Newark, New Jersey. While superintendent in Washington, D.C., Janey accomplished a significant victory by bringing the highly regarded Massachusetts education standards into D.C. schools. It was the right thing to do.

So the progress made under Rhee was due to Janey's groundwork? Look at it this way: to move the numbers in a school district such as D.C. is akin to assembling a two-hundred-piece jigsaw puzzle. Adopting new standards might amount to a handful of pieces. If imposing higher standards were the secret to achieving academic improvement, California would be highest-achieving state in the nation and Chicago would be the toast of urban school districts. Not the case; there's far more work involved.[9] Any school-by-school analysis during Rhee's term as chancellor reveals that the gains came from reforms that weren't happening under Janey. The academic advances made under Michelle Rhee were her gains.[10]

King also wrote a column suggesting that September 11, 2001, the day of the attacks in New York and Washington, D.C., was a day that marked the high point of academic excellence for D.C. public schools, an assertion that would leave any fact-checker sputtering. After the election, *Post* columnist Robert McCartney asserted that Baltimore's school chief, Andrés Alonso, had reached a Rhee-like teacher contract and was eliminating ineffective teachers but without all the drama created by Rhee when she did the same. That was an insight that appealed to future mayor Gray, who days later told Turque that he was an admirer of the Alonso school reform style. "I've been watching him." Problem is, Alonso didn't have a Rhee-like contract. He wasn't carrying out Rhee-like firings of ineffective teachers. And just to make things more embarrassing for the *Post,* not long after the column was written Baltimore teachers rejected Alonso's contract.[11]

The *Post* columnist most skillfully working the race angles was Courtland Milloy, who signaled that Rhee was firing teachers (the fact that most of the teachers were black didn't need to be spelled out) for no apparent reason— "roulette wheel" firings. (The actual issue was the fact that the layoffs were based on principal recommendation rather than seniority, which infuriated the unions.) Milloy painted an image of Rhee joyfully firing black teachers while cozying up to white Georgetown parents. In a postelection column that neatly summarized his pre-election opinion pieces on Rhee, Milloy referred to the Hardy Middle School controversy as he wrote:

> She has gone all out to make residents who live in the wealthier, predominantly white parts of the city feel good. And if their feathers got ruffled and needed smoothing, she went so far as to visit their homes for coffee klatches and pep talks.
>
> So what happens when black residents on the other side of town start waving their hands—don't forget about us; we'd like to feel good, too? Rhee holds them up for ridicule. School reform is not "warm and fuzzy," she says.[12]

Had Milloy e-mailed Rhee (who is famous for responding to e-mails within minutes or even seconds) he would have learned that she held more "living room" meetings in all-black Ward 8 than any other ward. But that didn't happen. At least on the Rhee story, I did not see the *Post* columns as being completely accurate. (Although when I asked Spayd whether *Post* columnists are fact-checked, she said they received the same editing as reporters.) Jo-Ann Armao rode to Rhee's rescue with an editorial refuting the race charge, pointing out that nearly all of Rhee's reform resources went to schools in low-income black neighborhoods. But then her rhetorical horse bolted:

> Any suggestion that Ms. Rhee lacks either passion for or interest in raising the achievement levels of black students—along with those of white, Latino, and special-education pupils—is a slander. The charge seriously misreads the past three years and 10 months and how Ms. Rhee has worked to fix a system that was notorious for its inability to provide textbooks to students, much less educate them.[13]

To readers, it appeared the *Post* editorial was responding to Milloy's earlier column printed in the *Post* Metro section; however, the correct word in that case would have been *libel*, not *slander*. Over the years, *The Washington Post* has turned in many "finest hours" of reporting. Its coverage of Rhee was not among them.

MORE FIRINGS—AND RETURN FIRE

For Rhee, the *Post*'s pre-election coverage was a nightmare, slipping into the racial politics she had been warned about when considering the job. At a critical point in Rhee's public relations freefall, Katherine Bradley, who runs the CityBridge Foundation social services nonprofit and is the wife of Atlantic Media owner David Bradley, stepped in to help. In spring 2010, it was announced that former Obama communications director Anita Dunn would guide Rhee on public relations strategies, courtesy of a grant from CityBridge. Dunn, a streetwise political advisor, held Rhee's hand as she navigated waters that always seemed to be morphing into uncharted rapids. Dunn could see that Rhee knew she had a problem. The controversial move to lay off 266 teachers, a story Rhee lost control over, chastened her. Rhee knew most of those teachers were low performers.[14] But once the *Post* Metro section steered the story toward her controversial magazine interview, the PR battle was lost.

Now, just two months before the mayoral primary, another round of firings loomed: the teachers deemed "ineffective" under Rhee's IMPACT teacher evaluation system. Though the timing couldn't be worse, Fenty told her to proceed. But how? She had nearly drowned in bad press over the last firings. Rhee knew she needed help and turned to Dunn. Here was one dilemma: everyone was going to want to know the number of teachers fired under IMPACT but it was complicated to quantify. Not everyone getting fired was a teacher. Some teachers had a theoretical possibility of getting hired elsewhere in the system. Others had the option of retiring to avoid being fired. There was no way to pin down an exact number of teachers getting axed.

Soon, Rhee and Dunn settled on a strategy: full disclosure. State the highest possible number of teachers that might be cut because if firings dribbled out over time, the press and union leaders would accuse Rhee of lowballing the number. "It was our feeling that this is a system that benefits from maximum transparency," said Dunn.

And so on July 23, 2010, Rhee released the news: 241 DCPS staffers would be subject to termination. Of those, 165 were being fired due to poor evaluations; the balance had credential shortfalls. In addition, another 737 teachers rated "minimally effective" under IMPACT were put on a one-year notice: improve or face dismissal. Said Rhee in a statement, "Every child in a District of Columbia public school has a right to a highly effective teacher—in every classroom, of every school, of every neighborhood, of every ward, in this city. That is our commitment."

After the announcement, Rhee and Dunn took deep breaths and awaited the blowback. What happened next startled even a veteran like Dunn. Although union leaders had a predictable reaction—AFT president Randi Weingarten referred to Rhee's "destructive cycle of hire, fire, repeat"—for the most part Rhee was drawing praise, at least nationally, for firing ineffective teachers. This was perhaps the first time any school chief got good press for firing teachers.

In Washington, D.C., Rhee's detractors seemed momentarily stunned. The first to recover with a public relations strategy was George Parker, the local union president. He claimed that Rhee was exaggerating the number of teacher firings in an attempt to make herself look like a firebrand reformer. Parker said he could find only 76 teachers fired for being ineffective, not 165.

The Metro section one-upped the teachers union by "discovering" even fewer teachers fired for poor performance.[15] Dunn and Rhee were astonished. The story angle they feared the most, accused of lowballing the firing numbers to avoid controversy, had flipped 180 degrees. Now they were being accused of exaggerating the number of teachers fired. "I didn't think anybody was going to accuse us of inflating the numbers," said Dunn, "because it seemed like such a ridiculous charge." Welcome to Rhee's world.

Rhee wrote a letter to the *Post* explaining the math behind the firings. A few months later, when the final count was in, the original estimate of firings came out almost exactly as Rhee had predicted, according to DCPS. But that didn't matter. The pre-election image of Rhee exaggerating the number of teachers she had fired had hardened (with many voters assuming these were mostly black teachers). Once again, Rhee got painted with the brush of joyfully firing black teachers.[16]

· · · · ·

For two years Rhee's opponents had been on the defensive, unable to successfully argue that the obviously failed system of the past was preferable to the progress Rhee was making. Given that black students benefitted the most from Rhee's reforms, turning race politics against her was a challenge. The Hardy Middle School controversy, combined with the racial flavorings of the firings, gave her detractors a unique opportunity to redefine Rhee's reforms: that she cared more about white students.

On the surface, the charge was silly. Only 7 percent of the students in the D.C. district are white and nearly all those bail out after elementary school. Rhee's major reforms targeted black schools in black neighborhoods. Her primary efforts to attract more middle-class families into the system, both white and black, involved small-scale preschool programs at a handful of elementary schools. But thousands of primary voters had been sold on another storyline: the rumor that Rhee's reforms favored whites sounded believable, and as the Ward 7 poll describes in Chapter Ten, it was believed.

Now was the time to recall the warning national school reformer Kati Haycock gave Rhee when she was considering taking the position: "The racial politics are going to be insane. You are going to get slaughtered." With the benefit of hindsight, it seems clear that the Hardy Middle School controversy is where the slaughter started. That was the point when her opponents redefined her. That was the point when, even though it didn't seem that way at the time, she was walking wounded.

Chapter Ten

THE MAYOR'S RACE

If any Washingtonians had a reason to reelect Adrian Fenty on September 14, 2010, it would surely be the voters filing into the polls at Anacostia's Sousa Middle School. Before Michelle Rhee took over the D.C. schools in 2007, Sousa was regarded as one of the worst middle schools in one of the nation's worst school systems. The halls were chaotic, the police were a constant presence, and few students could do grade-level work. But the principal Rhee appointed, Dwan Jordon, and his leadership team calmed Sousa's hallways and propelled test scores up a steep incline—all in record time and while the area was suffering economically. From 2007 to 2009, the same years Sousa's students were experiencing sharp gains, the poverty rate for black children in Washington, D.C., jumped from 31 to 43 percent.

In D.C., the Democratic primary is the de facto general election; Republicans here are a negligible force.[1] Given the rocky relationship between Rhee and challenger Vincent Gray, a Fenty loss in the primary would almost guarantee that Rhee would leave.[2] If that happened, the talent gathered at Sousa stood a good chance of being cherry-picked by other urban districts. Jordon was the highest-performing principal in the most-watched education reform experiment in the country. Especially with the release of the documentary *Waiting for "Superman,"* a star in Rhee's galaxy could write his ticket anywhere. Jordon's assistant principals could probably find principal jobs elsewhere. LaKeisha Wells, who had worked with Jordon in the Prince George's County schools and became Sousa's math curriculum coach, was responsible for helping teachers steer math instruction in the right direction. With that kind of success, Wells, who was later promoted to assistant principal, would be in demand at any school. Some of the teachers I interviewed came to Sousa because of Rhee. They wanted to be at the center of the nation's most ambitious school reform and were willing to work themselves to the point of exhaustion. But would they be willing to make the same sacrifices after the spotlight disappeared?

EXIT POLLING

Even with all that at stake, Fenty received only 76 votes at Sousa's Precinct 107, compared to 443 for challenger Vincent Gray. Frankly, I'm surprised Fenty pulled in that many votes. When I interviewed people leaving the polls at Sousa I didn't find a single Fenty supporter. Education reforms weren't the only things motivating these African American voters (many I spoke with thought Fenty had forgotten about the economic plight in the poor, black neighborhoods of Washington, D.C., such as Ward 7) but the school reform efforts rang loud—and not in a good way.

Conspiracy theories abounded: some were convinced Rhee's appointment smacked of cronyism (even though she had never met the mayor before she got the job). Most of all, people cited the teacher firings. Although they agreed that D.C. schools under Rhee were getting better, they didn't think it was necessary to fire teachers to achieve those gains.

"I don't appreciate anyone who causes people to fall into harsh times," said Bernice Blackwell. "They should have talked to the teachers and found out if they wanted to participate in this idea. They didn't ask. They just came in and cleaned them out. If I fire you and you're making top dollar, then I can bring in someone who's making less, so you're saving. I'm a parent who raised all her children in D.C. public schools. They didn't turn out bad. It's not the schools; it's the parents."

When Betty Morgan's children's teachers were fired, her kids came home crying. "I don't support Fenty, mainly because of the teachers," said Morgan. "When Michelle Rhee let them go, they were working good; they were good-working teachers. They were conscientious teachers. I didn't understand. When you hurt my baby, you hurt me."

"We're getting an influx of Teach for America teachers who don't have classroom experience, don't have classroom management skills, and are not certified," said Marvin Tucker. "I'm not here to say that all the teachers in the public school system were great, but the majority that were let go, they put in the time, they had the qualifications. Some had fifteen, twenty years of experience. They understood classroom management and teaching in an urban setting."

Why would you take someone's job away from them, I was asked, especially if the new teacher was no better than the old teacher? At one point a woman fluttered her hand in my direction and asked why *I* should be hired and a longtime teacher fired? What's to gain? I am white and I understood her to be referring to the mostly white Teach for America teachers some principals chose to hire in the hopes their energy would kindle the kind of fire the better Washington, D.C., charter schools had ignited. Those TFA hires, who actually didn't account for many of the new D.C. hires, were raised several times by the voters I interviewed.[3] One black magazine writer had referred to TFA hires as "cultural tourists" intruding on D.C., white folks with limited teaching skills absorbing the local culture and then fleeing the profession before they became accomplished.[4] The subtext was the same: why did you take away those jobs?

· · · · ·

To flesh out those sentiments I hired Clarus Research, a firm that had done several citywide polls about the mayoral primary, to conduct a highly targeted poll just in Ward 7, focusing as much as possible on the neighborhoods surrounding Sousa Middle School.[5] That poll, conducted a week after the primary, was designed to measure the politics of successful school reform. Did the Sousa turnaround orchestrated by Rhee make a difference?

More Ward 7 voters disapproved of the overall job Rhee had done than approved of it, 49 percent to 38 percent. Yet Ward 7 voters were equally split between those who said schools had improved and those who said they had gotten worse or at best stayed the same. Voters whose children attended Sousa were far more likely to say schools had improved; those who just said they were familiar with Sousa also said the school had improved because of Rhee, though by a smaller margin.

But even voters pleased with the progress didn't send that love Rhee's and Fenty's way. People did largely agree on one thing: 68 percent said the school system was in bad shape when Fenty took over and 58 percent said it was now moving in the right direction. Yet in question after question, people indicated that Fenty's education policies did not swing their votes his way, that Gray should not keep Rhee on, that the school reforms helped whites more than blacks, that all those teachers did not need to be fired.

Only 22 percent thought it was necessary to fire and replace Sousa teachers. (Among those familiar with Sousa, that number rose to 31 percent). Yet when I toured Sousa and talked with Jordon, teachers, and curriculum coaches, it seemed clear that keeping the old staff wasn't an option. That observation became even clearer when I visited schools nearby where principals haven't changed staffs that for years have consisted of the teachers no other schools would touch. In those places, proficiency rates in math and reading still linger below 20 percent. You'd think *that* would unleash a political backlash. But that's not what got voters at the Sousa precinct angry. Reform did, at least reform that involved firing teachers. Mayors beware.

FENTY'S SHORTCOMINGS

Michelle Rhee is hardly the only reason Fenty lost the Democratic primary. People found him aloof and arrogant—a technocrat who assumed that improvements in schools, playgrounds, and the crime rate would speak for themselves. He didn't conduct polls; he ignored advisors. Why spend time working black churches and attending funerals? To black voters in D.C., Fenty turned out to be the quintessential postracial mayor in a city that was far from postracial, especially in the midst of a deep recession. The most telling example: on the weekend before the primary, while Gray was working his way through three black churches, Fenty participated in a triathlon.

Fenty's appointments, in a city that for decades had been run by blacks, included a white police chief and the first non-black schools chief in anyone's memory. When Rhee began firing central office staff and teachers for incompetency, those firings (unavoidably) involved African Americans. This violated the legacy of D.C., a government-dominated city without a manufacturing base, where public-sector jobs were the most reliable ladders into the middle class. The *Post* interviewed one voter who echoed what I heard outside Sousa: "He fired those teachers, that did it for me," said Wilson Givens, a retired, black equipment operator who lives in Anacostia, in southeast, who voted for Fenty in 2006. "Does he understand that a job is a family's livelihood? I don't know anybody who was fired personally, but I can relate. I know how it feels, and I felt for those teachers and their families. That was it for me. Would never trust him again."[6]

In the end, Fenty won fifty-three of the city's majority-white census tracts, but only ten of the majority-black tracts. Gray won 108 of the majority-black tracts, but just five that were majority-white.[7] After the election, Fenty blamed his loss on the radical school reforms, a path he said he'd choose again. Rhee's reforms, he said during a television interview after the election, made D.C. "the leading edge of a movement. . . . If it's a war, someone's got to be at the front of the line, and they've got to get killed first. That's how you win a war, is by going forward."[8]

· · · · ·

The repeated clashes he and Rhee endured with local and national teachers unions, which supported Gray, cost him at the polls, Fenty said. "The teachers unions aren't bad per se, but the teachers unions are going to have to explain why when every tough decision is made to reform the school system they are at the lead in opposing it. . . . If you are going to be at the front of the line in preventing reform, then I believe that the bad outweighs the good."

By my political reckoning, Fenty's loss had more to do with race than union opposition. Fenty may be black, but on primary day he became the "white" candidate. I'm guessing the American Federation of Teachers could have spent $1, rather than (possibly) $1 million, to defeat Fenty and the outcome would have been the same.[9] In Washington, D.C., attitudes toward school reform were sharply divided by race. While I was hearing anger at Rhee from Sousa voters, across town, Allison Tierney, a white mother of three from Tenleytown in northwest Washington, D.C., told *The Washington Post* that she voted for Fenty because of Rhee's reforms, and was pleased with the teacher firings. "Most of them probably needed to be let go," she said. "They were there too long, and they needed a change."[10] White voters thought Rhee was cleaning house; black voters saw no reason to sweep out a head of household with a steady paycheck.

Even more damning, many black voters, as illustrated in the Ward 7 poll, thought Rhee was favoring white families. Those twin impressions—favoring whites and firing black teachers for no reason—were fanned by *Post* local columnists and greatly helped Vincent Gray, who nurtured those impressions by referring to his brand of school reform as one that would involve all the "stakeholders." It was not hard to read meaning into that term. Teachers who felt they had been abused by Rhee were a key member of the stakeholder club supporting Gray. At the top of their worry list were the 737 "minimally effective" teachers whose jobs were at risk in 2011. Gray also vowed that his administration would reach out to the forgotten wards, especially Wards 7 and 8 in Anacostia. It wasn't hard to read meaning into that, either. Unlike Fenty and Rhee, he would not favor the whites.

· · · · ·

One person who witnessed the racial overtones was Sacramento Mayor Kevin Johnson, who is engaged to Rhee.[11] In the run-up to the primary, the former NBA star came to Washington, D.C., to campaign on behalf of Fenty, knocking on doors in Wards 3 (mostly white) and 5 (mostly black) and making appearances in Anacostia neighborhoods. "I'd knock on a door and these ladies would answer and say they weren't going to vote for Adrian Fenty." When pressed for a reason, the topic of school reform usually arose quickly. "They would acknowledge that Michelle had done a good job and the schools were better but they'd take it farther and say they didn't feel like they were listened to."

In American communities, says Johnson, the issue of respect always bubbles close to the surface. "If we don't trust what's being done, then this potentially becomes another experiment on our community. . . . If you had to boil it down to one word it would be *respect,* when you are listening to us and you are hearing what our issues are and you are taking the time to explain why you're doing what you're doing so you are building your case. I think [Fenty and Rhee] could have done a better job with that."

The commonly held perception in black neighborhoods that Rhee cared more about white families was "preposterous," says Johnson. "If that were the case, she never would have come to D.C. to run the school system. She's a fighter for the underdog; part of that came firsthand from Baltimore. As a teacher she saw these African American kids and the injustice of our education system. That's what really drives her crazy." Johnson agrees that the teacher firings (and Hardy Middle school; see Chapter Nine) fueled the conspiracy theory only because most of the D.C. teachers are black. "In cities around the country, like in D.C., the black middle class are educators, they're teachers, they're principals. So when you have a tough economy they are impacted in a disproportionate amount. I think that parlayed into a race issue. Whether it was right or wrong, it became real because you're talking about people's livelihoods in a real way."

· · · · ·

Gray expertly played off those with fears with his "One City" campaign theme, which suggested that Fenty and Rhee had forgotten the black neighborhoods. It worked and that's just the real world of politics. In this case, however, the politics of a winning campaign could cripple future school reform. Both while serving as council chairman and running for mayor, Gray did his best to thwart Rhee's campaign to weed out ineffective teachers. On primary day, that put him on the winning side of the issue—pulling in the votes of those who thought Rhee favored whites.

Yet Gray had to know that the reason Sousa Middle School, located in his own ward, was able achieve a dramatic turnaround was that almost every teacher in the building was replaced. Gray had to know that Rhee deserved credit for the improvements during the 2009–10 school year at his own alma mater, Dunbar High School, a school that before Rhee took over had descended into a kind of chaos most of us can't even imagine. Not until Rhee brought in Friends of Bedford and cleaned out more than half the staff did Dunbar become safe for students and teachers.[12]

With Rhee gone, will Gray level with his supporters about what really needs to happen in D.C. schools? Or will he keep the lessons of Dunbar and Sousa to himself? It is politically risky, in this case, to be honest. It is also the right thing to do.

Chapter Eleven

LESSONS LEARNED

A sk any of the many Michelle Rhee detractors in Washington, D.C., to list the mistakes she made during her tenure as chancellor and you are sure to hear the following: She foolishly tried to fire her way to success. She was oblivious to race sensitivities and kowtowed to rich, white Georgetowners so they'd send their children to the public schools. She needlessly humiliated teachers and principals in reckless interviews with the national press. She devised an evaluation system designed solely for punishment, and she refused to collaborate.

Winners earn the privilege of interpreting history and so it will be with the new mayor. That means all those complaints listed previously, coupled with an even longer list, will be cited as Rhee's shortcomings. However, other than teachers' union leaders, there are few national education experts who don't consider Rhee's D.C. reforms to have been the most important recent education experiment in the country. It took twenty years of thrashing about before school reformers finally settled on teacher quality as the key ingredient behind improving student performance. And nobody pushed the teacher quality reforms harder, faster, and more effectively than Michelle Rhee. Everyone wants to know: did the Rhee reforms work?

Answering the question of what went right and what went wrong first requires sifting through the competing story lines that define Rhee's work in Washington, D.C. The American Federation of Teachers, for example, which (possibly) invested $1 million in defeating Fenty and ousting Rhee, wants to ratchet down her success in D.C. so that other school chiefs don't start demanding the same kind of tenure-weakening, performance-based contracts that Rhee won—and that weaken the reason for belonging to a union. Their message to those who might seek to emulate Rhee: this, too, can happen to you if you mess with the unions. The reformers and foundations that embraced Rhee's teacher-quality take on school reform have their own storyline to push. They want D.C. to serve as the national model to fuel a school reform revolution based on marketplace incentives to improve teacher performance. Their message to school chiefs: Michelle Rhee and her reforms *are* the pathway to success.

An analysis of Rhee's three-and-a-half years in D.C. breaks down into three categories: what she did right, popular-but-flawed myths about her attitudes and actions, and her actual shortcomings as schools chancellor.

What Rhee Did Right

Assessing Rhee's shortcomings starts with the clear victories. In less than four years Rhee straightened out a horrendous back office that couldn't count students, deliver textbooks, distribute meals efficiently, keep school boilers working, track student performance—pretty much everything a central office is supposed to do. She closed underused schools that were devouring the district's budget and seized control of a special education system that had been so badly managed in the past that it had been turned over to judges to run. Rhee's sophisticated teacher evaluation system, IMPACT, makes the systems used by most districts look like crude starter kits. Teachers that were shortchanging students actually got fired—something that other school chiefs, even the reform-minded ones, have failed to do. "Rhee has publicly challenged the status quo and has shamed anyone in education that isn't putting the needs of kids first," said Susan Schaeffler, who runs the city's high-performing KIPP charter schools. "She has fired teachers and closed down schools that have been abusing the public education system and made it clear that there is no place to hide and collect a paycheck in DCPS anymore."

Finally, Rhee accomplished the unimaginable: in only three years she moved the student performance numbers significantly upward on the gold standard of tests, the federal National Assessment of Educational Progress (NAEP). "NAEP is not a test that is calibrated to produce large jumps," said Michael Casserly from the Council of the Great City Schools, a top expert on urban school reform. "The gains she made on NAEP between 2007 and 2009 were pretty unusual. In fact, her reading and math gains in both fourth and eighth grade were as good or better than any other city over the same period," Casserly said. NAEP wasn't the only shining point of data. A month after the primary, when it was too late to do any political good, it was announced that enrollment in D.C. public schools had increased, for the first time in four decades.

Popular Mythology

Rhee's purported shortcomings fall into two categories: wrongs that are more public perception than reality (myths) and actual failures. Let's look first at the myths.

Rhee never learned to collaborate. True, Rhee once famously asserted that "cooperation, collaboration, and consensus-building are way overrated." Nobody ever forgot that line, especially Vincent Gray, who said during his campaign that school reform does not have to be a blood sport and vowed to restore collaboration to the D.C. schools. Rhee had delivered that oft-cited line to a summit of public policy officials during her second year on the job. She explained later, "If collaboration is the most important thing in your end goal, the only way to make a whole lot of people happy is to not change anything. But if you want to change things, the fact is there will be a group of people mad at you."

School closings put that principle to the test.

In May 2006, then-Chancellor Clifford Janey held a press conference to announce that he wanted to close six schools. That took the deputy mayor for education, Victor Reinoso, by surprise, because he expected a larger number. Janey had told Reinoso that half the D.C. schools were underused and twenty schools needed to be shut down to steer budget dollars back to educating students. But when it came down to it, Janey decided that, in light of opposition from community groups and the teachers union, getting unanimous approval from the school board was more important than closing as many schools as they needed to.[1]

Reinoso pressed Janey. "As long as you get a majority of the votes it doesn't matter what the minority thinks," he told him. "You're backing off a difficult decision in order to make what would have been a 7:2 or 8:1 vote unanimous. You're compromising your agenda for the sake of this appearance of consensus."

But Janey stuck to his decision. He didn't "want to upset the applecart," Reinoso said.

In the end, Janey managed to close five schools. Rhee, by contrast, closed twenty-three schools immediately. Comparing Rhee and Janey on school closings is not totally fair. Rhee had a power that Janey lacked: mayoral control of schools. Comparing them on approaches to compromising with elected officials, however, is fair. Janey, unlike Rhee, insisted on full buy-in. Rhee, for example, could have informed councilmembers before she announced the closings. Given that they were about to get peppered by constituents furious about the closings, that would have been a politically wise gesture of collaboration. Nearly every other school chief in the country would have briefed the council. But Rhee never tried to reach consensus with the council because she suspected they would seek a way to derail the closings. A safe bet.

In the short term, Rhee got her schools closed. In the long term, of course, she lost. The snub to the council over school closings was followed by clashes over teacher firings and the budget, which were followed by Vincent Gray deciding to challenge Fenty, and winning.

Does that prove Rhee was wrong about collaboration being overrated? That's debatable but one thing is certain: the next schools chief in D.C. won't have a couple dozen practically empty schools draining the budget.

Rhee was a cold-hearted bully. Among Rhee haters, this allegation usually took on a racial flavor. Wrote *The New York Times* columnist Bob Herbert after Fenty lost his reelection bid:

> Mr. Fenty was cheered by whites for bringing in the cold-blooded Michelle Rhee as schools chancellor. She attacked D.C.'s admittedly failing school system with an unseemly ferocity and seemed to take great delight in doing it. Hundreds of teachers were fired and concerns raised by parents about Ms. Rhee's take-no-prisoners approach were ignored. It was disrespectful.[2]

Herbert nicely summarizes the Rhee complaint. She did seem cold-blooded. Why else would she agree to appear on the cover of *Time* looking like a heartless scold? Let's be honest: this complaint has legs. Rhee not only sacked the admired principal of her daughters' school, but she also fired a principal with the TV cameras running. To many Washingtonians, the votes against Fenty were payback for Rhee (and by extension, Fenty) being a bully. After the election, *The Washington Post* columnist Courtland Milloy wrote a piece originally headlined: "Ding-Dong, Fenty's Gone. The Wicked Mayor Is Gone." Rhee, Milloy wrote, "spit in our faces."

True, Rhee could be fierce and rude. "I will cut you off if you're not making sense or it's not a good use of my time," she says. She went out of her way to exclude councilmembers from the decision process. Plus, she constantly picked fights. Forget about the unions. She even got into fights with her supporters.

When TFA founder Wendy Kopp, a close colleague of Rhee's, sat down with me for an interview, her eyes got big as she described Rhee's combativeness. "She will stand up and just go after even her greatest allies in reform," she said.

Rhee is supportive of charter schools and their leaders. But one day, talking to me, she teed off on some of D.C.'s elite charter operators. They were afraid her new pay package, which offered higher salaries than charters did, would lure their teachers away. Rhee told me, "I was thinking, are you for real?" Her voice got cold and low as she talked about the years the charters had taken advantage of D.C.'s "crazy bureaucracy" to pluck the best teachers away from DCPS. "But when we start to get competitive, they want to shut down the competition. These people want school reform until it starts impinging on their own self-interest." She was furious. And these were her friends.

To look at Rhee's fierceness, however, and conclude that bullying defines her personality is naive. How could Rhee have built The New Teacher Project into a major player in education reform, persuading scores of school superintendents to hand over part of their teacher recruitment, without exhibiting diplomacy? Anyone who believes Rhee can't be personable has never talked to her colleagues or watched her run a staff meeting. The point to make is this: she knows when to switch off the charm. The latter is what happens when you do something she thinks is not good for the kids; that's the Rhee on the cover of *Time*.

After all, charm only goes so far. Take Education Secretary Arne Duncan. Everyone agrees he is charming, a likeable, self-effacing guy who as Chicago schools chief got along with everyone, from neighborhood groups to the unions. That, in part, explains why President Obama tapped him as the nation's top educator. Don't get me wrong. In Chicago Duncan made a lot of tough decisions that most would agree were for the better. And he has done an admirable job as secretary of education. But here's the difference between nice-guy Duncan and bully Rhee: Duncan never got his students' NAEP scores up; Rhee did.[3]

Rhee was obsessed with drawing more whites into the schools. On election day, as interviews showed, this perception killed Rhee. Along with the view that she needlessly fired older black teachers who defined Washington, D.C.'s middle class, this shaped Rhee's image and explained why her approval ratings among black female voters hovered at a mere 25 percent. It's not difficult to identify the sources of this complaint. It starts with Hardy Middle School (Chapter Nine), where middle-class black families roared in anger over her proposed changes.

Similar themes emerged in other neighborhoods—Capitol Hill, Adams Morgan, and Foggy Bottom—as DCPS began offering new preschool programs in these mixed-race, middle-class neighborhoods where many families had long forsaken the public schools. The idea was to hook the families young and keep them there as their children progressed into the upper grades. Rhee wanted to alleviate schools' racial and economic isolation—a goal liberal groups usually promote—and draw in more activist parents likely to attend back-to-school nights and demand higher standards. Any other urban school district in the country would rejoice at the idea of middle-class parents embracing the local schools. And in

Washington, D.C., a city whose white population is increasing, reaching out to white families would seem not just logical but imperative.

In this city, however, it was seen by many black voters as signs of dreaded gentrification. Or, more simply put, a not-so-subtle message to move elsewhere. That feeling was exacerbated by the reality that that most of the teachers Rhee fired for being ineffective—firings she seemed passionate about—were black. On primary day, black voters delivered a clear message to both Rhee and Fenty: *you* move out.

That Rhee was on the wrong side of the election ballot, though, is not the same as being on the wrong side of principle. DCPS, as much as any urban school system in the nation, needs to draw more middle-class families, no matter what their race.

Rhee focused too much on teacher quality. When I first started researching this book, that was my instinct. Why did Rhee talk constantly about teacher quality and nothing else? What about curriculum reforms? In 2009, as a journalist working for the Broad Prize for Urban Education, I visited successful districts around the country.[4] In Long Beach, California, officials created a math program, invested thousands of hours training teachers how to use it, evaluated how well they implemented the program, devised a program to help teachers overcome their shortcomings, then invested thousands more hours retraining the teachers to do an even better job. It was an inspiring and exhausting process to watch. In Aldine, Texas, and Broward County, Florida, I watched teachers quickstep through test-and-teach, test-and-reteach maneuvers designed to prevent students from falling behind. At Aldine Ninth Grade School, for example, "lost" credits from either failures or poor attendance were treated by teachers as a kind of scavenger hunt: let's seek out students slipping behind and rescue them. Students faltering in algebra, for example, simultaneously take catch-up and regular courses rather than the deadening remedial courses that drive up dropout rates. In Gwinnett County, Georgia, I saw a school district construct—and then follow in dance-contest precision—exacting learning standards. If Rhee was supposed to be rescuing D.C. schools, and these districts were the best of the best, why wasn't I seeing any of these fast-paced curriculum reforms in her schools?

Once I started visiting schools and interviewing education experts, the answer became clear: the school system Rhee inherited was a full ten years behind one like Long Beach. D.C.'s data systems were in disarray. Rhee had no way of measuring even something as simple as attendance; the idea that she could immediately implement the quick-turnaround diagnostic testing used by these celebrated districts was a fantasy. And data systems weren't even the biggest deficit she faced. Long Beach had a decade-old system for hiring teachers who would prove effective from their first day in the classroom, many of them trained at nearby Long Beach State University by school district officials acting as instructors. Aldine had built an equally effective teacher corps by drawing on a network of contacts with the nation's best teacher-training facilities. Gwinnett was swamped with applications from the state's best teaching candidates: the result of success spawning more success.

In D.C., by contrast, Rhee inherited a teacher corps of 4,500, only about a third of whom were capable of executing the kind of rocket-science teaching seen in Long Beach.[5] That left Rhee's academic advisors with limited options. Matching a curriculum to a very limited workforce would mean bringing in a teacher-proof, by-the-book instructional program such as Open Court Reading. Michael Moody, Rhee's academic advisor, and others on the Rhee team were wary of that strategy; if students didn't learn, teachers could blame the script. "Part of what we wanted to do was change the mindset of teachers, to get them taking ownership," said Moody. "We wanted to remove all the excuses and say at the heart of this is that teachers can impact achievement regardless of the circumstances."

D.C. already had strong curriculum standards. Teachers in every grade knew what their children were *supposed* to learn in that school year. They just weren't doing it effectively. So Rhee's team focused on changing the quality of instruction. This strategy appealed to the band of Teach for America reformers who surrounded Rhee; it mirrored what she had done in Baltimore and other team members had accomplished in their own difficult teaching assignments: use powerful teaching to reach kids.

The task of rebuilding D.C.'s teaching force fell to top Rhee aide Jason Kamras, who had been named national Teacher of the Year while teaching math at Sousa Middle School. Surrounded by a mostly flailing student body, Kamras constructed a tiny oasis of learning in his class, just as Rhee had done in Baltimore. Kamras recalls reaching his most disruptive student through playing chess, a suggestion he got when soliciting advice from the boy's mother. "I think he was wondering why this crazy teacher wanted to play chess with him but he did sense I cared about him," Kamras said. The student went on to become an engineer; they still stay in touch.

Now, Kamras would be tasked to infuse D.C.'s teaching force with *snap,* that style of teaching you can recognize immediately just by peeking into classroom doors of the country's best schools. To move D.C. teachers in that direction, Kamras devised IMPACT, a tool that the teachers' union scorns as a punitive evaluation model but is better described as an exacting teaching model. Following these precise steps, IMPACT says, will lead to both good evaluations and improved student learning.

Only a handful of school districts in the country have a program as sophisticated as IMPACT, says Michael Casserly, the urban schools expert. Said Brad Jupp, a top advisor to Arne Duncan who negotiated an innovative pay-and-evaluation system when he was a union official in Denver: "It is an excellent blend of precisely described excellent teaching behaviors and fair administrative procedures for making judgments about teaching performance." The teacher evaluation part of IMPACT, when individual teachers are observed for up to nine hours, leads to tailored professional development advice. "It is an exercise in profound professional realism," said Jupp.

As much as I admire the school reforms in districts such as Aldine and Long Beach, in the end I concluded that Rhee placed the early emphasis exactly where it belonged: boosting teacher quality through IMPACT.

Rhee arrogantly claimed that only *she* put kids first. Nothing infuriated Rhee's critics more than listening to her claim that she was right because she put the interests of kids first. The implication: if you disagree with my methods, you don't care about the children. Time after time, that standoff left her adversaries sputtering with rage. Logic suggests Rhee is wrong. Of course it's possible for two parties to disagree about what's best for kids. Interestingly, Rhee never really seemed to get why that made so many people angry, which reveals something about her.

But for a moment, let's look at this from Rhee's perspective. She jumped into an environment in which everyone quickly claimed that they were keeping kids' interests at the forefront—and then proceeded to pursue their own agenda. Rhee, meanwhile, tried to filter decisions through a single lens: is this good or bad for kids? At times this backfired politically and it certainly hastened her departure. But in reporting on Rhee's time in D.C., I find myself hard-pressed to think of a single decision in which she veered from her true north. How could the Washington Teachers Union officials be putting kids first when they tried to fend off thorough evaluations of teachers? How could parents be putting kids first when they fought to keep open empty, lousy schools? How could councilmembers be putting kids first when they tried to reverse the firings of ineffective teachers? Considering that low-income black students in D.C. were as much as two years behind their peers in other cities, how could any of that be in the best interests of children?

Saying "this is best for the kids" about things that weren't was so common to Washington, D.C., culture that Rhee's critics never understood—and still don't—that she was not being cynical. Shortly after Fenty lost his reelection bid, Rhee appeared at D.C.'s Newseum for a screening of *Waiting for "Superman."* During a discussion after the movie, Rhee said the election results were "devastating" for schoolchildren, which kicked off another media frenzy. Was she insulting Vincent Gray by suggesting he would hurt kids? Why was she even bringing kids into the debate? Gray demanded to know.

Rhee later explained, in a letter to the *Post,* that she meant that the election was "devastating" if people took it to mean education reforms should be reversed. Still, I had to laugh. To me, her private thoughts were spilling out. Gray had been challenging Rhee's reforms for several years. His strongest supporters were her biggest detractors. The American Federation of Teachers had put major money into Gray's campaign because they wanted Rhee and her reforms to disappear. She had every reason to worry that Gray would find ways to shift her reforms into neutral at best and even maybe reverse. And from her perspective that meant putting adults first, kids last. To her way of thinking: devastating.

Rhee felt so strongly about the student-first issue that she chose it as her next career move, launching the Student First organization that essentially takes her D.C. fight over this to a national level.

Rhee was too quick to get rid of principals and teachers. It can't be denied: *Rhee was ruthless.* During a nearly four-year period, roughly half the DCPS teaching staff turned over (a combination of layoffs, resignations, and retirements) along with a third of the principals, most of whom were fired.[6] In the highest-performing urban school districts in the country, places such as Long Beach, Aldine, and Montgomery County, Maryland, such numbers would be frightful. In fact, the next head to roll would belong to the schools superintendent. So why should Rhee get a pass?

Let's start with what Rhee found when she arrived in 2007. Remember, at that time, D.C. schools were tied with Los Angeles as the worst school district in the country. Finding the problem didn't require sophisticated sleuthing: it was a lack of teaching and learning in the classroom. D.C. teachers, long considered the most important element of the city's black middle class, were in fact not helping the very children to whom they had dedicated their lives. And far too many hapless principals were doing nothing to correct the problem. As best as I can determine, neither the principals nor the teachers were even aware of this dilemma; most assumed the poor outcomes were caused solely by factors they had no control over: poverty and single-parent families. Rhee felt she had to act.

With principals, Rhee's solution was a rapid remove-and-replace campaign. As explained in Chapter Seven, Rhee's rules for principals were short and sweet. If you were assigned an out-of-control school, you had one year to restore calm. Get the hallways safe, the bathrooms monitored, the truancy under at least some kind of control and, most important, reestablish respect for authority. Fail at that and you're sacked. If you succeed at regaining control, you have another year to rekindle teaching and learning. Fail at that and you're sacked.

That's the theory. In reality, the success of her principal replacements hinged on the quality of the replacement pool. Rhee's reputation as an urban crusader attracted a surge of applicants who wanted to prove themselves in the D.C. spotlight. "The problem is we have extraordinarily high standards," Rhee says. So that big pool shrinks quickly. If that final list of those who pass muster is too small, principals who are still struggling to get control of hallways, or still struggling to shift from hallway control to teaching and learning, get a year's grace.

Further complicating the principal turnover issue were the hires that didn't work out. A new principal Rhee picked to run Spingarn High School for the 2009–2010 school year allowed the high school to spin out of control, with rowdy students roaming the halls smoking dope, setting fires, and breaking into classrooms to intimidate both students and teachers. Not until a teacher e-mailed Rhee directly did she become aware of the chaos. Rhee arranged a faculty-only meeting at Spingarn. "All the teachers I met with had the right attitude, were very nice, but were scared that someone might eventually be killed at the school because the kids were out of control." Rhee immediately replaced the principal and takes the blame for hiring an ineffective leader. "I wish I batted 1.000 on principals," she said, "but I don't."

Was Rhee's system fair and effective? Hard to say. I wouldn't want to be held to those standards. When I visited Johnson Middle School only moments after Principal David Markus learned he was fired for failing to seize control of the school (see Chapter Seven), he was hurt but philosophical. A single year is just not sufficient to turn around a school in this kind of shape, he told me. After touring the school, I had to agree with Markus. It's hard to imagine a mere mortal living up to that demand.

Did that make Rhee wrong? Rhee kept churning through principals because she saw some, such as Dwan Jordon at Sousa, achieve what was supposedly unachievable. When talking about a persistently failing school,

Rhee would use successful principals as examples: Jordon would have found a way to move out lousy teachers. Jordon would have found a way to filter out all distractions and focus solely on teaching and learning. And Jordon wasn't an outlier; other principals in the system were performing similar feats. If they could do it, Rhee reasoned, so could others. So it was just a matter of finding a sufficient supply of "others" to take the helm at D.C. schools—which was no sure thing.

The teacher firings are an easier call. I found nothing to dispute the calculation that only a third of DCPS teachers were able or willing to get students at least on par with minority children in other urban areas. D.C. illustrates the national research documenting the sad decline of teacher quality over recent decades, as the best and brightest women took advantage of more attractive jobs opening up to them. As measured by class rank, admissions scores or teacher certification test scores, the quality of teaching applicants, especially in urban schools, declined significantly. Rhee may have been scorned for her teacher firings, they may have helped Fenty lose the election (and it may be brutal and politically incorrect to say this) but the reality is that she fired too few teachers, not too many.

RHEE'S TRUE MISSTEPS

Someone with a reputation as a world-class debater, at least when measured by persistence and endurance, would usually be a person hesitant to admit mistakes. I found Rhee surprisingly open to discussing her missteps. How will future school chiefs avoid my mistakes if they can't identify them? she told me at one point.

Rhee failed to create public buy-in for the reforms. Described in the simplest terms, Rhee's core mission was to shift D.C. schools from an adult-centered system to a student-centered system. Doing that successfully, however, requires convincing the adults they need to sacrifice for the children. "You need a broad sense across the community that we're all in this together to improve the school system—a sense of, 'Can you work with me to make all this happen on behalf of the kids?'" says Michael Casserly. During Rhee's years in D.C., that never happened. As was made clear on Election Day, too few voters saw Rhee's vision as meriting sacrifice. So who's to blame?

First in line, ironically, is Adrian Fenty, who appointed Rhee, blessed her with a boosted budget, won her the power to fire whom she needed to, and never once flinched when her reforms veered in politically costly directions. Those were huge sacrifices for which Rhee will be forever grateful and are the reason you will never find Rhee agreeing with what I'm about to say: Fenty screwed up. It was Rhee's job to rescue D.C. children; it was Fenty's job to convince the adults to make sacrifices. "In many ways I thought Fenty was an extremely good manager but rather a tone-deaf politician," Casserly says. "It's really the job of any political leader to help shape, guide, and define public expectations. . . . I think he could have helped build public buy-in and ownership for the reforms in a way that he did not do."

Maybe Fenty assumed the obvious school improvements—the renovation of dilapidated buildings, test score
gains, a surge of talent from around the country wanting to
teach or lead schools—would speak for themselves. Instead
of proactively explaining the layoffs and firings and trumpet-
ing the improvements, Fenty either left Rhee on her own or
reacted only on the defense. Rhee hesitated to step into Fenty's role, so she was left to do her own PR. And those who saw
the *Time* cover know how successful that was.

That could have been overcome, says Anita Dunn, the
former White House political advisor who stepped in to
help Rhee. "People had to feel good about the progress D.C.
schools were making without having to like Michelle Rhee,"
Dunn says. "When people's feelings about the D.C. schools
become a referendum on her, then it's hard to accept the
good things even when they recognize the good things." It's
like when I interviewed voters emerging from Sousa Middle
School, one of the most striking urban school turnarounds
I've ever seen. Rhee got no credit for any positive develop-
ments there. All that was on anyone's mind were teacher
firings, which they didn't think had anything to do with
school quality.

Fenty's lapses became Rhee's lapses when she failed to
recognize what was playing out. At that point, she should
have been more proactive or insisted on more from her boss.
Instead, Rhee stayed hunkered down, explaining reforms to
local residents in the same language she would use at a think
tank, if she explained them at all. "I think we know from
long experience and long observation that especially in black
communities, process matters a lot," says Kati Haycock of

Education Trust, a Rhee supporter. "Respect matters a lot. Elders matter a lot. And neither she nor the mayor was attentive to that."

Had Rhee been more attentive and Fenty more proactive, would that have been enough? Based on what I heard from voters on primary day, I'm doubtful. The disdain for Rhee's reforms was about jobs. In the midst of a recession and gentrification pressures, seeing DCPS employees fired struck many voters as black removal and no explanation could have convinced them otherwise.

Rhee fought battles that didn't need fighting. The school closings certainly damaged Rhee. People are attached to their neighborhood schools, even if they only have one hundred students. In fact, they consider that a good thing. The school closings (see Chapter Five) did real damage to relations with D.C. councilmembers: they wound up looking both ignorant and helpless. Mayor Fenty famously abused councilmembers on many levels, including the most trivial: refusing to dole out passes to the council for access to seats in the government's suite at the new Nationals baseball stadium. But when it came to schools, Rhee could have mitigated the hostility. She could have briefed members the day before announcing the school closings. She could have treated testimony at their hearings as something other than a forensics competition.

Rhee couldn't get past what she saw as hypocrisy among some councilmembers. They would agree in private that the district was wasting money maintaining too many schools but then publicly condemn closings in their ward. She says that even though councilmembers knew the teachers she laid off due to a budget shortfall were poor performers, they pushed her to hire them back. But hypocrisy has always been part of the repertoire of successful politicians. Why should Rhee be surprised and offended? Why should she invite retribution by disdaining the council the same way the mayor did? Inevitably, the political brushbacks added up.

Hardy Middle School (Chapter Nine) is another battle that didn't need to happen. Rhee's logic for making those changes was impeccable. It made sense to try to bring more Georgetown families into the system. But Hardy Middle School was the wrong battle at the wrong time.

Rhee made some terrible media judgments. For the moment, let's set aside that awful *Time* cover. Stuff happens, especially when you're brand-new at being a national figure—and when you aren't accompanied on photo shoots by savvy PR professionals. That's not how Rhee rolls. She makes her own way around the world, relying on her own counsel. But as the months passed, it became clear that this was a reckless habit. Consider the interview with *Fast Company* magazine, where she said that among those laid off during a budget trim were teachers who had hit or had sex with children. That was a gift to Rhee's opponents. Rhee protested that she was quoted out of context. Perhaps, but the more relevant question to ask is, why was she talking to a business magazine about the firings in the first place? It's safe to say the readers of *Fast Company* are not the parents in the black wards of D.C., the people she really needed to be selling her reforms to.

Most astonishing was the anything-goes access she gave PBS education correspondent John Merrow, whose cameras followed her through the day. In his book *Below C Level*,[7] Merrow recounts his surprise one day as Rhee told his crew: "I'm going to fire somebody in a little while. Do you want to see that?" As Merrow points out, the word "see" means only one thing to a film crew: she was going to allow them to shoot her firing a principal. And that's exactly what happened, with Rhee saying, "I'm terminating your principalship—*now*." Oscar-winner Davis Guggenheim used that video in his documentary, *Waiting for "Superman,"* thus guaranteeing a wide audience for the firing.

The fact that the cameraman shot from behind the principal, obscuring his or her identity, was almost irrelevant. Talk about disrespect. There's no way to weigh Rhee's action that day and reach any conclusion other than it was thoughtless and reckless.

There's a lot I've come to learn and admire about Michelle Rhee but I have never understood why she persisted in giving national interviews that always hurt her in D.C. Rhee says there was an upside to the press coverage, especially in that it helped attract foundations willing to commit millions to teacher pay-for-performance bonuses. And the publicity drew in talent—teachers and principals wanting to prove themselves in the media spotlight. "It has also caused me a significant headache, for sure," she says.

Given the gush of positive national publicity Rhee has received, outsiders often compliment her on her "amazing PR machine," which makes Rhee laugh. "Are you kidding me? We're a bunch of amateurs sitting around. We had no clue, no strategy. It just happened to us." At one point she asked a writer for *Washingtonian* magazine why she drew so much press attention and he answered, "Because you give good quote. You will say the things that no other public official will say." It's true. I first heard Rhee speak at a D.C. event where she described the incompetent employees she had discovered at the central office—in graphic detail. This was of the kind of honesty that reporters crave and, at least from educators, rarely get. But in interview after interview, only Rhee's most biting comments got used. Over the months, it killed her but she realized that too late. "Now I understand why people I have great respect for stick to their talking points and never waver from them," she says.

Not that Rhee will ever stick to a memo and speak in bland platitudes, even after her boss was clobbered in the election. Unvarnished directness—that's something she got from her mother.

Rhee drove out (some) good D.C. teachers. There were plenty of D.C. teachers who believed in Rhee's reforms, including many of the "highly effective" teachers eligible for bonuses up to $25,000. After nine years they could make an annual salary of $130,000, compared to $87,500 after twenty-one years in the old system. But there were too many teachers who didn't buy in. The Washington Teachers Union so disliked Rhee's IMPACT teacher evaluation system that they refused to support her application for U.S. Department of Education Race to the Top funds. (The city won $75 million anyway.) Union antagonism is to be expected; the problem arose from alienating some effective teachers.

One "highly effective" teacher who sat on one of Rhee's advisory councils recalled listening to Rhee in the national press say that teachers were the source of urban school problems.[8] To this teacher, it sounded like Rhee was including teachers like her who put in long hours and rarely got home before 7 p.m. Rhee recognizes the problem. She knows she should have made sure that her teacher effectiveness message never sounded hostile to top teachers. "Whenever I talk about teachers to press people, I always talk about how we have great teachers but that is never the part that gets quoted," Rhee said. "I could only say the good things, so there are no out-of-context quotes, but that omits the bigger picture. I think it's important to talk about the reality that we have some bad teachers and we have to get rid of them. So I think it is unfortunate that people like that hear the messages and think it is being targeted to them because that is not my intention."

In hindsight, Rhee says she made the same mistake that as head of The New Teacher Project she counseled superintendents against making: allowing others to define you. "I told superintendents not to abdicate the responsibility of communicating to the rank and file, to the union . . . but that is exactly what I did." The union and the media ended up shaping the message. Any way you parse it, Rhee lost some good teachers.

Rhee's team came up short on school supports. In the highest-performing school districts, teachers tap into district-provided, online toolboxes for help with just about anything. Through those resources, the teachers are told not only exactly what skills to teach, but they also are given a pacing guide that tells them how to time their instruction.

From those Web sites teachers can pluck lesson plans crafted by master teachers. Plus, the teachers have access to quick turnaround diagnostic tests that make clear which students are absorbing the lessons—and which students need to be retaught specific skills.

When Rhee arrived in D.C., the district had solid learning standards but not much else in the way of academic supports. The system was about a decade behind successful districts when it came to functioning data systems, diagnostic tests, vetted lessons plans—well, you name it. Although Rhee took steps in that direction, her efforts bordered on the frantic. And inside schools, that desperation showed. "Too many cooks in the kitchen," one experienced academic coach described it.

That coach, who asked to remain anonymous, worked with several failing schools that faced reconstitution, when a school is either taken over by an outside operator or completely scoured for an academic restart. This coach saw several problems. Multiple branches of the central office bombarded schools with multiple training programs that at times were in conflict. Teachers got ground down by all the mandatory form-filling-out meetings. And teachers never got what they really needed: a curriculum designed to meet the standards with pacing guides and expert lesson plans. "There were never enough concrete lessons for teachers to use," Kati Haycock said. "If you're starting with a labor force as low level as that one, the only thing you can do in the short term is increase the rigor of assignments by giving them better ones to use. I think Rhee could have had a better chief academic officer, with more resources and supports there, from the beginning."

Rhee is quick to agree that D.C. schools remain a chasm apart from high-performing urban districts such as Long Beach and Aldine. "If Aldine is a 10, we are far from a 10. Now, did we bring D.C. up from 0 to 3? Yeah. But we still aren't anywhere where we need to be." In 2007, when Rhee took over, she found a school district barely able to tie its own shoes. Sorting out data systems that didn't work, closing unneeded schools, delivering textbooks—all those took time. Building the IMPACT teacher professional development system took even more time. "So, if you ask me if I had prioritized differently, could we be an Aldine by now? I don't think so, not based on where we were when I arrived."

Perhaps not, but the heavy lifting on curriculum reforms now falls to her successors.

Chapter Twelve

WHAT'S NEXT?

About two weeks after the primary I interviewed Michelle Rhee in her DCPS office for the last time. I arrived at 2 p.m. to find her working both her phone and her Black-Berry. On her desk was a fat, greasy paper bag stuffed with fries. No burger, just fries. Inches away rested a jumbo cup-cake smeared with thick frosting. All untouched. She may have been too busy to eat but that's what she aspired to con-sume for lunch. That distinctive combination of work inten-sity and unabashed gusto is why, despite being shunned by most Washington, D.C., voters on primary day, Rhee is likely to continue to be a force in education reform.

This isn't to say her reforms will live on. As council chairman, the new mayor, Vincent Gray, was unremittingly hostile to Rhee's reforms. And the Washington Teachers Union has a new president, Nathan Saunders, elected in part because he bitterly opposed the very air Rhee breathed. Saun-ders was the enthusiastic choice of The Washington Teacher, the dissident teachers blog (written by Candi Peterson, who ran as Saunders's WTU vice president) that portrayed Rhee, literally, as a witch. When she announced her departure, the site ran an image of the Wicked Witch of the East crushed by Dorothy's house—all that showed were the red shoes and striped stockings.

As for Rhee's many D.C. supporters—those who voted for outgoing Mayor Adrian Fenty mostly because they thought Rhee was giving their children a first-ever shot at a decent education at a local, traditional public school—their views about her have not changed. Nor have their fears about what Gray will do to reward his many anti-Rhee backers. In winter 2010, as I close out the narrative of Rhee's tenure in Washington, D.C., it is premature to predict the direction Gray will take. But one can still draw conclusions about Rhee's legacy in D.C. and beyond.

THE D.C. LEGACY

Walking from D.C.'s Union Station to the headquarters of D.C. schools takes less than ten minutes; it's a trip I made many times while researching this book. In early spring 2010 during the first weeks of my research, I never looked forward to that walk. I'd take the Metro to Union Station and then sit in the Amtrak waiting area, pretending to be boarding a train. Then, fifteen minutes before my interview time I'd launch out along First Street, sidestepping panhandlers, enduring construction sites that guaranteed deafening noise and clouds of dust, and then passing by the Greyhound bus station and its sad men with glazed eyes. The school headquarters was a modern office building located in a place where you couldn't catch a cab or buy a cup of coffee to go.

By the time my research project wrapped up, however, that walk had changed dramatically. Some of the construction wrapped up, revealing sparkling office and apartment buildings, restaurants and sandwich shops, and the crowning glory for this neighborhood: a Harris Teeter grocery store, located right across the street from DCPS. Unlike cities such as Detroit, where urban renewal is nearly dead, Washington, D.C., is being gentrified, a process fueled by the bounty of government-connected jobs. That change is reflected in the city's demographics. In 2000, the city was 61 percent black and 34 percent white. By 2008, D.C. lost twenty-seven thousand blacks and gained forty thousand whites, reducing the black majority to 54 percent. By 2020, D.C. is likely to cease being a black-majority city, an unsettling vision for the city's poor, black population.[1]

On primary day in 2010, the vast majority of those black voters lined up against Adrian Fenty, someone they had come to see as the pro-gentrification, postracial candidate. Fenty being out of office, however, will slow down neither gentrification nor the population shifts. The question is whether D.C.'s schools will become a positive part of the city's future. In theory, D.C., where more than a third of public school students attend charter schools, could continue to drift toward being an all-charter district. That's not what Fenty had in mind when he took over as mayor. D.C. has several high-performing charter schools but the overall record for charters has not been outstanding. As a whole, traditional D.C. elementary schools outperform them. So neither Fenty nor Rhee, despite Rhee's close affiliations with top charter groups, believed the city could rely on charters as a strategy for improvement. The most successful charter groups, Rhee explains, are trying to build their own districts. "You can't have individual schools out there all buying their own health insurance and meals and buses and all, so by necessity you need something that operates as a mini district. You need a centralized capacity to be able to do quality control." In other words, you need exactly what Rhee tried to do with DCPS.

The top charter school leaders don't disagree with the need to maintain and improve the regular schools. "Even with a robust charter school system in D.C., we still have a need for the traditional school system," says KIPP's Susan Schaeffler. "D.C. residents value the concept of school choice. The intent of the charters wasn't to eliminate the traditional schools but to work side by side offering parents and students more options to choose from. Rhee's attitude toward charters has been, if you can do it better than us, then do it."

· · · · ·

Building a school district to compete with the best charters, of course, was easier to set as a goal than to actually accomplish. The reality that Rhee inherited in 2007 was a majority-black city sharply divided by race. D.C. lacks the sizable working-class white population found in many cities and most of the professional-class families, white and black, remove their children after elementary school, leaving behind a racially and economically isolated network of middle schools and high schools that have proved themselves to be spectacular failures at preparing students for any sort of professional future.

Turning around DCPS involved thousands of moving parts and a two-pronged strategy. First, vastly improve all-black schools located in wards unlikely to ever experience economic or racial diversity. Second, attract more white and black middle-class families into schools in transitional neighborhoods. The first task, centered mostly in neighborhoods east of the Anacostia River, consumed the vast majority of Rhee's time. It relied on a blunt-force tactic: bringing in unflinching reformer-principals or outside "partners" experienced at school makeovers. Rhee made this work in some schools. Dunbar High School, for example, at least stabilized and showed some academic progress (Chapter Eight). Sousa Middle School has improved more dramatically (Chapter Seven).

Will the first part of her plan, seeking more outside partners and aggressive reform principals, outlive Rhee? Probably. The only alternative is to return to the pre-Rhee years when D.C. schools tied for last place nationally. Whether this approach can endure, though, depends on how much backlash political leaders are willing to stomach. Under the old contract, teachers fired by one principal were guaranteed jobs elsewhere in the system. That meant that while the reformer principals at Dunbar and Sousa got what they needed, other city schools got stuck with their rejects. With the new contract signed in 2010, however, those teachers are not guaranteed jobs elsewhere. Good news? Only on the surface. Spreading the aggressive reform from school to school and backing strong principals means tolerating more teacher firings, the very action that many black voters rejected during the primary.

· · · · ·

The second part of her plan—drawing more professional families into the D.C. school system—is one in which the gains are vulnerable to quick reversals. Once these parents conclude the district threatens their children's future, they vanish almost overnight. You only have to walk a few blocks from D.C. schools headquarters to get a glimpse of this. A preprimary walk through the NoMa (north of Massachusetts Avenue) neighborhood, home to J.O. Wilson Elementary School, revealed scores of rehabbed row houses and a smattering of young white families with strollers parked on the front porch (and often with Fenty posters in the yard). Makes sense; long-gentrified Capitol Hill is a reasonable walk away and there are two close-by Metro stations. Less obvious to someone walking by are the black middle-class families willing to give Wilson a try. One of those mothers was Samantha Caruth, who in 2009 moved to Washington, D.C., from New York City, where she had worked as director of admissions for a private school. Her husband enrolled in a PhD program and she worked as the head of career counseling at a nearby university. In 2010 they had a son in third grade and a daughter in kindergarten.

In D.C. they bought and renovated a house in NoMa about three blocks from Wilson, a school where 96 percent of the students are black and 91 percent qualify for free or reduced-price lunches. Despite the racial isolation and poverty, Wilson does a better job than most D.C. elementary schools: in 2009, when the Caruth family was considering Wilson, 71 percent of the student met or exceeded the district's standards in reading, 76 percent in math. Still, they had hoped for a school with more diversity and higher academic standards, similar to what they'd found in New York schools. They applied to more diverse D.C. schools outside their neighborhood, as well as a charter school, but couldn't find spots for both children. In the end, based partly on the confidence they had in Rhee's reforms, they decided Wilson was their best bet.

Is Wilson giving their children what they need? "This is a daily conversation my husband and I have," Caruth told me. "We made a very strategic decision moving into this neighborhood. We chose this school because we were going on faith and we had a good first impression. We also know that you can't put these kinds of things on cruise control." Caruth joined the executive committee of the PTA board, which helps them stay in touch with the school staff. And they were happy when, in the middle of the year, the principal got rid of one of their daughter's teachers, whom they thought was weak. But they were disheartened that on back-to-school night, only about a fourth of the parents in their son's third-grade class showed up—a measure they view as insufficient parent engagement. Rhee leaving makes them "extremely nervous. . . . She's the one who delivered on a school district that everyone else neglected." But for now, they're committed to keeping their children in the school because they feel like the progress at their school can't help but endure. "We're hopeful that the change that Rhee has put in place over the last three years will continue to bear fruit."[2]

·   · · · · ·

Across town, software entrepreneur Mona Sehgal and her husband, Philip Hagen, were taking a different kind of chance on the Francis-Stevens Education Campus, where nearly 90 percent of the students are black and close to 70 percent qualify for free and reduced meals. At this pre-K–8 school in 2010, only 40 percent of the students met standards in math and 45 percent in reading. The school is located on the edge of a very upscale neighborhood, with fancy hotels and offices only a block away. Few of those neighbors send their kids to Francis-Stevens; nearly all the children are "out of boundary" applicants. This was one of several schools where Rhee launched a preschool program designed to pull in families from the immediate neighborhood, hoping they would persist through the later grades.

Sehgal, who is of Indian descent, has a son in preschool and an infant daughter. She has lived in this Foggy Bottom neighborhood for seventeen years and had set up a life that revolves around walking everywhere, including to work. She had been driving her son to a preschool in another neighborhood, but rush hour in Washington, D.C., a city that sometimes exceeds Los Angeles in the amount of time wasted in traffic, was too much to bear. Sehgal was intrigued by the new early education program Rhee launched at Francis-Stevens and became the organizer for a group of parents considering the new preschool. Rhee came to the school several times to discuss the initiative. "I think the support from Rhee was important and the fact that she was there and behind the school is important," said Sehgal. "That could sway some people but I think in the end it comes down to do you feel comfortable sending your child there? So it's not Michelle Rhee; it's the teachers."

For the 2009–2010 school year, Francis-Stevens opened up two preschool classes, with fifteen children each—including Sehgal's son. This is an educated group of parents and most of them are happy about their decision, says Sehgal. Will they stay? "Everyone is taking it year to year," said Sehgal. "They are looking all over. Other D.C. schools, private schools, the suburbs." Sehgal hesitates to predict how those decisions will turn out. Parents worry more about the interactions between children and teachers than about who is mayor or schools chief, she said. The one development that could change minds rapidly, said Sehgal, would be a decision to bring back teachers who were fired "for cause," a demand Gray hears from his supporters.

Although Rhee's two strategic approaches were very different, their chances of survival come down to the same issue: will Vincent Gray continue the tough push on teacher quality? Rhee opponents, especially the teachers' unions, worked hard to elect Gray and poured money into his campaign. They might assume their battle is won and that eventually, Gray will move to dilute Rhee's teacher reforms. To date, however, Gray has said nothing to indicate he would do that. And he named Kaya Henderson, Rhee's close friend and deputy chancellor, as the interim chancellor, which is encouraging.

HAD THERE BEEN FOUR MORE YEARS

If Gray retains Henderson as chancellor—and if he chooses to continue Rhee's reforms—the next four years of D.C. school reforms under Henderson may resemble what Rhee would have pursued. But even working with that by-no-means-certain scenario as a starting place, we are left with the question of where Rhee would have taken D.C. schools. A few weeks after her resignation I spoke with Rhee about what might have happened—under ideal circumstances—had she stayed. She said that the emphasis on teacher quality would have continued but she hoped the teacher turnover rate would have stabilized. "You would have a teaching force that had lived through the performance pay system. They'd actually have money in their pockets so they'd know it was real. I think it would make the best people want to stay and attract great new teachers. Through IMPACT, we would have removed the lowest performers and professionally developed those who need to improve their practice. As a result of those two things—rewarding the best and moving the others up or out—four years from now we would have one of the strongest teaching forces of any urban district."

If the teacher force stabilized, so would the turnover of principals, she said. "With the new contract, we now have an environment in which the best teachers have incentives to stay and ineffective teachers can be removed and aren't owed jobs elsewhere. We would have principals from around the country saying they would love to come to work here because they would have the ability to staff their own school with the people they knew could impact student achievement."

The push to draw in more middle-class families, black and white, would have picked up speed, said Rhee. "We're bringing more compelling and rigorous programming into our schools: preschool, pre-K, foreign languages, International Baccalaureate. When those programs grow and thrive, they will compel families to come into DCPS and stay there." The slight uptick in enrollment in D.C. schools, the first in forty-one years, would have been followed by slight increases, she predicted. "About three or four years from now, when all these reforms matured, you would have seen that enrollment line move a little bit more."

One move that would have triggered more clashes with the council would have been asking for authority to launch charter schools within DCPS. "I would go to D.C. Prep, E.L. Haynes, KIPP, and other great charters in the city and ask them to take over some of our failing schools. The outside partners we have contracted with to take over some of our schools are still limited a bit in their authority and autonomy. They have to hire people through our HR department, that kind of thing."

But would the council have granted that authority to Rhee? "There would be opposition, probably from the people who believed that Michelle Rhee was orchestrating the demise of public education in this country. They would see the move toward charters as privatization."

The National Legacy: Grasping for "Michelle Lite"

Listen to other school reformers talk about Rhee and it comes down to one message: we plan to do what she did . . . only without all the drama. Michelle Lite, if you will. That certainly appeals to Gray, who shortly after the primary asserted that he was an admirer of Baltimore's Andrés Alonso, a schools chief he believed was getting Rhee-like changes absent the drama. Other school superintendents are seeking the same kind of milder reform. Only days after Rhee announced she was leaving D.C. schools, she appeared at a national meeting of the Council of Great City Schools in Tampa. "Be prepared to be Ms. or Mr. Unpopular," she told the urban school administrators. "I am really good at this one right now." But not everyone there was planning to be unpopular. At another presentation, the superintendent of Hillsborough County, which includes Tampa, outlined a Michelle Lite strategy. MaryEllen Elia told the school chiefs she was "absolutely" opposed to the tough line Rhee has taken on low-performing teachers. "We're coming from a different approach on the same issue," said Elia, whose district had received a $202 million grant from the Bill & Melinda Gates Foundation to build a teacher evaluation system that she said would put more emphasis on mentoring and professional development.[3]

. . . . .

It sounds so appealing: Michelle Rhee, without all the drama. Who would oppose that? Dipping into the details, however, is sobering. In Tampa, Elia estimated she would have to eliminate only 5 percent of the district's tenured teachers in the initial years of the reform. Rhee, meanwhile, inherited a district in which at most a third of the teachers were capable of handling sophisticated reforms, with or without professional development. As for Gray's vision of Alonso in Baltimore, that was never anything more than a mirage. Alonso never negotiated the kind of tough teacher-accountability system Rhee won in Washington, D.C.

Those awkward facts, however, don't mean that all urban districts need to launch the kind of scouring that occurred in D.C. If districts such as Hillsborough need to separate only 5 percent of their teachers, Michelle Lite is possible. Not all urban schools are the same, although they tend to get lumped together. In reality, urban districts sort into three groups. In the bottom group are districts such as D.C., Baltimore, Detroit, Los Angeles, and St. Louis—the worst performers that need a complete overhaul. Too many years of hiring teachers incapable of moving children forward have taken a toll. For these districts, focusing solely on curriculum reforms would be a wasted effort. The next group of urban districts—including Miami-Dade County, Florida; Atlanta, Georgia; Fresno, California; and St. Paul, Minnesota—has somewhat better teachers and a good start on the data systems and curriculum reforms that can lead to success. The top group of urban school districts, such as Long Beach Unified School District outside Los Angeles and Aldine Independent School District outside Houston, enjoy a steady supply of high-quality teachers and are thereby able to focus solely on the kind of professional development that assists those teachers in using their fast-paced, effective teaching programs.

The gulf between these groups is immense. At least ten years of progress separate the school districts in the top and bottom tiers. So the Long Beaches in the top tier don't need to take lessons from Rhee's work in Washington, D.C., but the other groups have plenty to learn, and what they need to pay attention to is this: teacher quality must be the top priority. During her time in D.C., Rhee fired about four hundred teachers for being ineffective educators. That's about 390 more than similar urban districts each managed to fire. For Rhee, finding teachers with *snap* paid off, at least on educational measures, with federal test scores rising significantly. Politically, of course, it backfired and Fenty and Rhee lost their jobs. Which lesson will the bottom-dwelling districts take away: that culling the teaching force is imperative or that firing teachers will get you fired? The answer, I'm guessing, depends on leaders' resoluteness. How badly do they want schools that work?

Many people think cities have too much riding on improving education to hide. Rhee's fiancé, Sacramento Mayor Kevin Johnson, for example, laughed when I asked him if the political loss in Washington, D.C., would intimidate other education-reform minded mayors and governors. "Around this country there's a sense of enough is enough about schools, a sense of outrage." Evidence of that, he said, is seen in the heavy recruitment Rhee experienced after announcing she was leaving D.C. schools. "I have never seen anybody, other than a LeBron James or Kobe Bryant, more highly recruited than Michelle is right now. This is not an exaggeration. I'm talking governors, coast to coast, mayors from major cities, foundations, universities . . . everything you could imagine. So when you ask the question of whether the appetite for school reform is there, the answer is absolutely."[4]

That surge of offers aimed at Rhee, however, raises the question of whether her recruitment merely reflects the fact that she's a rarity, unlikely to be duplicated in other school districts. Considering the many troubled urban school districts, that's an ominous thought. "My basic take on Michelle is that if her fortitude and tenacity are what's required to really change these systems then the kids are in big trouble," said Andrew Rotherham, cofounder of Bellwether Education and creator of Eduwonk. "She did what most people can't or won't. On all the big changes in D.C., one commonality was Michelle hanging tough until the last dog died. It's a story of tenacity. And in that way it's profoundly depressing given the scale of the problems in so many places. Waiting for more Michelle Rhees to come along will be a long wait." Perhaps. But those same mayors and governors trying to recruit Rhee have to know the political trouble they are inviting. And if they don't land Rhee they'll look for a Rhee substitute with the same agenda of pushing for dramatic boosts in teacher quality.

. . . . .

Two stories about the quality of teachers and principals stand out from reporting this book. The first was Rhee's description of what happened when she started to fire central office employees for offenses such as botched special education paperwork that cost the districts hundreds of thousands of dollars. The initial legal advice she got: around here, we don't fire people for mere incompetence. We just transfer them to the schools. Think about that for a moment and then multiply it by a decade—or two or three.

The second story was one I heard in an interview with a D.C. schools advisor working with several failing schools to help them improve and perhaps avoid reconstitution. She described seeing teachers just let students putter around the classroom; no planned lessons. In another of the failing schools she ran up against a principal whose top priority was to maintain "workplace ease" for her teachers. Translated, that means fending off outsiders offering advice how to improve instruction. A curriculum coach who showed up in a classroom found herself the subject of a nasty note from the teacher to the principal: keep this person out of my classroom; this violates my workplace ease. Just telling the stories about these two schools made the advisor agitated. The problem with these low-performing D.C. schools, she said, lies with many of the teachers and principals. "It's not the kids!" she half shouted. "There's nothing wrong with the children!"

She's right—it's not the kids. There's only one reason poor black kids in D.C. are as much as two years behind similar children in many other urban districts, and it has nothing to do with the message of the Slowe sign and everything to do with its being posted in the first place.

Looking Ahead

In December 2010 Rhee appeared on "Oprah" (and secured a cover essay in *Newsweek*) to reveal her future: Students First. "I am going to start a revolution," Rhee told Oprah. Her immediate goal was attracting one million supporters and $1 billion in funds in the first year. "We have textbook manufacturers, teachers' unions, and even food vendors that work hard to dictate and determine policy. The public-employee unions in D.C., including the teachers' union, spent huge sums of money to defeat Fenty. In fact, the new chapter president has said his No. 1 priority is job security for teachers, but there is no big organized group that defends and promotes and interests of children."[5]

Children First will operate on two levels, Rhee explained: the practical and the political. On the practical level, for example, Rhee wants to export many of the D.C. reforms to interested school districts, especially the IMPACT evaluation system and the unique pay package she won that ties pay to effectiveness. "I don't think that every school district should have to reinvent the wheel." Referring to reform-minded school districts, she said, "We all think we have to create our own contract, whereas the union is not creating new contracts with every fight. They get a template from the national office."

On the political level, Rhee will draw on hard-learned lessons from Washington, D.C., where she and Fenty won education progress but lost votes. "We need to create an environment where politicians who are taking courageous stands can actually have some political backing. One of the things we know with this mayoral election is that the union played a huge part here, both in terms of money and boots on the ground, getting people to the polls, all that stuff, which is fine. So in my opinion the reform community should have had an equal effort, or even more."

As Rhee sees it, Students First will get involved when there's a political fight around school reform, doing everything from getting voters to the polls to organizing parents who approve of politically controversial reforms. "In D.C. we never effectively mobilized the parents who actually liked what we were doing to stand up and say that."

In short, Rhee plans to take the D.C. fight national, which means showing up in multiple cities with an innocent-sounding message packed with explosive implications: it's not the kids.

NOTES

PREFACE

1. Daly would take over as president of The New Teachers Project.

2. Former D.C. Schools Superintendent Clifford Janey appeared in an education forum with mayoral challenger Vincent Gray and challenged Rhee's premise about teacher quality. Just 13 percent of a child's academic progress can be attributed to the classroom, he said. The balance rests in the family and community. "Janey: It's Not a Coup," Bill Turque, Washington Post blog. http://voices.washingtonpost.com/dcschools/, April 1, 2010. (Janey declined repeated invitations to be interviewed for this book.)

3. Duncan disputes this characterization, saying he appeared with Rhee more than any other local school leader, which, if you count ceremonial appearances such as school safety walks, is undoubtedly true.

4. Teach for America, founded by Wendy Kopp, is a national corps of recent college graduates, usually from highly selective colleges, who commit to teach in urban or rural public schools for two years.

5. Amacom, 2010.

INTRODUCTION

1. As the project journalist for the 2009 Broad Prize for Urban Education, I wrote about districts imposing reforms, such as the International Baccalaureate, on a student feeder pattern (elementary to middle to high school). Lacking a predictable feeder pattern, D.C. school chiefs can't draw on that reform option.

CHAPTER ONE

1. Michelle's older brother, Erik, owns a real estate brokerage firm in Denver. Her younger brother, Brian, appears on radio and television shows in Korea that promote learning English. Michelle jokingly describes him as a "C-list celebrity" in Korea.

CHAPTER TWO

1. Rhee said she was working off what her principal told her. "Back then, it wasn't like you were given reports on how well your kids did. It's not anything close to how things are now. Basically, we were told by our principal: your kids made etc., etc. So we just took that as the truth. When I talked about the kids going from the bottom to the top, it's not like I was saying that based on nothing. It was what our principal told us. Again, it was a different era in terms of what was given to teachers in terms of the evidence or proof."

2. That model, known as Tesseract, did not prove to be successful in Baltimore.

3. Rhee does not recall this.

4. Rhee recalls being told about the vote altering but chose not to challenge it. The other teacher in contention was a veteran teacher at the school. "Finally I said she should win. I made it a nonissue."

CHAPTER THREE

1. Public Affairs, 2001.

2. In 1994 Linda Darling-Hammond, then a professor at Columbia University, published an article in *Phi Delta Kappan* entitled "Who Will Speak for the Children?" The piece questioned the TFA track record and concluded the group's shortcomings were so serious that TFA recruits were harming districts. The accusation (and research) by Darling-Hammond underwent intense scrutiny. In the following years other research would show a positive impact TFA teachers were having on children. Among scores of education reformers, many of whom are TFAers, Darling-Hammond's piece was neither forgotten nor forgiven. When Barack Obama tapped her as an education consultant, and it was assumed she was headed to the U.S. Department of Education for a major role, the harshness of the criticism directed at Darling-Hammond astonished many observers—and reinforced the cultlike image of TFA. Darling-Hammond withdrew from consideration for an administration post.

3. I have witnessed Rhee's considerable appetite myself. Often, when I would show up to interview Rhee at her office, around 1 p.m., we would talk over her lunch.

Invariably, her lunch would have fed a stevedore: a huge slab of meatloaf and mashed potatoes comes to mind. At another interview she had a large-size McDonald's sweet tea and three round plastic tubs of food: potato salad, macaroni and cheese, and red beans and rice.

4. Persistently failing schools can be reconstituted, which means, in its most severe terms, hitting the restart button—new staff and curriculum. To avoid school-year disruptions, reconstitutions are done in the summer, which results in releasing those teachers into the assigned teacher pool right before school starts.

5. The AFT and Weingarten refused to discuss any issues regarding Rhee, as explained in Chapter Six.

6. Guided by those who know Michelle and Kevin well, I concluded the divorce was not a player in the story I'm telling. The two cooperate closely to raise daughters who have turned out well. Therefore, I never pursued the personal issues behind the divorce.

Chapter Four

1. Simon & Schuster, 1994.

2. Ibid., p. 266.

3. Rhee appointed Wilhoyte to oversee a cluster of schools. Under Rhee, Wilhoyte's wife, Cheryl, took over a D.C. elementary school.

4. I was able to hire Mills thanks to grants from the Broad and Kaufman foundations.

5. In 2003, ten urban districts were compared. In 2005 and 2007, eleven districts were compared.

6. "Why Great Teachers Matter to Low-Income Students," Joel Klein, Michael Lomax, and Janet Murgia, *The Washington Post,* April 9, 2010.

7. Janey declined to be interviewed for this book.

8. Armao became a firm supporter of Rhee's reforms on the *Post*'s editorial page She declined to be interviewed for the book.

9. "D.C. Mayoral Race: With Grit and Diplomacy, Gray Pushes Through Agenda," Tim Craig, *The Washington Post,* Aug. 20, 2010.

10. Rhee served on the board of the charter school organization Johnson started in Sacramento, prior to running for mayor. In 2008, their acquaintance turned into a romance.

11. In January, 2011, Sandman announced he was leaving DCPS to take over the federal Legal Services Corp.

12. After Rhee left DCPS, Henderson became interim chancellor.

13. In December, 2010, Tata announced he was leaving DCPS to become superintendent of the Wake County, N.C., school system. As of January, 2011, Rhee's key academic team was still intact, but departures were considered likely should Henderson not stay as chancellor.

CHAPTER FIVE

1. Washington has eight wards but is more logically divided by Rock Creek Park. Neighborhoods west of the park, such as Ward 3, are where prosperous whites live. The wards east of the park are mostly black and

Wards 7 and 8 east of the Anacostia River, the portion of the city known as Anacostia, are the poorest.

2. "Angry Parents Question School Closings," Theola Labbe, *The Washington Post,* Dec. 4, 2007.

3. "For him, the issue of closing schools was never about racism but about lack of equal opportunities in communities that need it most," said spokesperson Victoria Leonard.

CHAPTER SIX

1. "Schoolyard Brawl," Evan Thomas, *Newsweek,* March 6, 2010.

2. Speech supplied by the American Federation of Teachers.

3. Speech supplied by District of Columbia Public Schools.

4. From the AFT's perspective, I would be an example of the national press naively buying into that cynical and simplistic argument.

5. Bullock and her union collaborators went through $5 million of union money: a $50,000 silver flatware set snapped up on the union American Express card along with a catered wedding and Washington Wizards tickets. Said Bullock at her trial: "I like china. I like crystal. I like shoes—you name it."

6. I was unable to confirm this with Weingarten because in fall 2010 Weingarten's staff cancelled a scheduled book interview with me after, at their insistence, I sent them a list of questions I intended to ask. Soon after the list of questions arrived, Weingarten declined to be interviewed.

7. "Rhee Seeks Tenure-Pay Swap for Teachers," V. Dion Haynes, *The Washington Post,* July 3, 2008.

8. Ibid.

9. A spokesperson for Parker never returned a confirmation request.

10. Rhee insists she had no clue when DCPS hired more than nine hundred teachers that her budget would soon be cut. "We thought our budget was protected because it passed." I found no evidence suggesting otherwise. A few DCPS officials said they were aware that was a possibility but with budgets that's always possible, they said.

11. "Update: Michelle Rhee vs. the D.C. Teachers' Union," Jeff Chu, *Fast Company,* Feb. 1, 2010.

12. "The Education Manifesto," Michelle Rhee and Adrian Fenty, *Wall Street Journal,* Oct. 30, 2010.

13. The 266 teachers laid off were a mixed bag. Some good teachers got laid off, said Rhee, usually because they were teaching a subject that was being phased out or working in a school with falling enrollments. And although the firings came before Rhee could get a good read on teachers from the new IMPACT evaluation system, she had profiles of the teachers from principals and the old evaluation system. Most of those laid off, she says, "were people you would not want in your child's classroom."

14. AFT negotiator Rob Weil agrees the firings had a profound impact on the teachers. What few people realized, including many of the teachers, is that D.C. chancellors already have unprecedented powers to fire

staff, he said. AFT negotiators couldn't negotiate away those powers, which is why many mistakenly concluded after the contract was approved that Rhee had won too much. Those unusual powers are why the D.C. contract will never be a domino contract likely to spread to other districts, he said.

15. "Math, Science Teachers Get Paid Less Than Others," Donna Gordon Blankinship, Associated Press, Aug. 18, 2010.

16. New York has had far greater success with its efforts to deny tenure to ineffective teachers during their probationary period. In 2005, just twenty-five new teachers were denied tenure, less than 1 percent of the pool of probationary teachers. By 2009–2010 that figure shot up to 234 teachers, or 11 percent of the pool.

17. "LAUSD'S Dance of the Lemons," Beth Barrett, *L.A. Weekly,* Feb. 11, 2010.

18. If firing senior teachers is hugely time-consuming because of union regulations, the preventative approach is identifying teachers as incompetent and removing them *before* they have earned their tenure. Usually that means in their first three years. But this doesn't happen, either. In Chicago, 87 percent of probationary teachers received either "superior" or "excellent" reviews, according to The New Teacher Project, which also found that two-thirds of the probationary teachers in the areas that they surveyed received a rating greater than satisfactory. Although it's easy to scapegoat unions as the barrier to removing ineffective teachers, here the onus rests squarely on principals and the districts that train them.

19. In 2009, education consultant Andrew Rotherham
    and I wrote a commentary for *The Wall Street Journal*
    that carried the headline, "How Teachers Unions Lost
    the Media." Even liberal bastions such as the edito-
    rial page of *The New York Times* had turned on the
    unions, we pointed out. And the usually ultraliberal
    New Yorker published a scathing piece on New York's
    infamous "rubber room." Soon after that commentary
    hit the streets, Rotherham and I got pounded by AFT
    officials. How could we print such fantastic untruths?
    But as time has shown, those observations were neither
    untrue nor fantastic. Today, newspaper editorial boards
    regularly rake the unions with criticism, usually over
    the issue of protecting bad teachers. In summer 2010,
    when the prospect arose of tens of thousands teachers
    across the country getting laid off for budget reasons,
    editorial writers mostly drew the line: Congress should
    not give states a nickel unless the unions agreed to
    abandon their last-hired, first-fired provisions, which
    ensure that young but effective teachers get the axe
    before older teachers who may or may not be better.

20. "Despite Guggenheim's undeniably good intentions,
    the film falls short by casting two outliers in starring
    roles—the 'bad' teacher as villain, and charter schools
    as heroes ready to save the day. The problem is that
    these caricatures are more fictional than factual . . .
    The plain, unsexy fact is that the best way to improve
    teacher quality is to do a better job of developing and
    supporting the teachers to whom we entrust our chil-
    dren's educations." "Saving Our Schools: Superman

or Real Solutions?" Randi Weingarten, *Huffington Post,* June 28, 2010.

21. "D.C. Teachers' Union Ratifies Contract, Basing Pay on Results, Not Seniority," Bill Turque, *The Washington Post,* June 3, 2010.

22. The Ballou teachers rated effective had three options: a $25,000 buyout, early retirement (for those with more than twenty years of experience) or an extra year (during which they were assigned temporary teaching positions) to find another school willing to take them permanently. If they couldn't find another job within the year, they would be terminated. The minimally effective teachers had sixty days to find another job. The Ballou teachers rated ineffective were terminated.

23. "Rhee's Appearance at D.C. Mayor Fenty's Rally Shows Disregard for Law," Courtland Milloy, *The Washington Post,* Sept. 6, 2010.

CHAPTER SEVEN

1. In some cases, a successful "lockdown" principal still gets removed because he or she is not considered the ideal school leader to take the school to the next step. That appeared to be the case at Dunbar High School.

2. "In District's Ward 8, Economic Recovery Is a World Away," Dana Hedgpeth. *The Washington Post,* June 13, 2010.

3. We Shall Overcome, Historic Places of the Civil Rights Movement. National Park Service. http://www.nps.gov/nr/travel/civilrights/

4. Jordon's first year, the 2008–2009 school year.

5. Jordon says the teacher went out on medical leave and never returned.

6. "There's No Such Thing as a Reading Test," E. D. Hirsch and Robert Pondiscio, *The American Prospect*, June 13, 2010.

7. "D.C. Principal's Hands-on Tack Transforms Sousa Middle but Also Ruffles Feathers," Stephanie Mccrummen, *The Washington Post*, July 6, 2010.

8. The Washington Teacher promoted the candidacy of Washington Teachers Union vice president Nathan Saunders against WTU president George Parker. In November 2010, Saunders defeated Parker and became president.

CHAPTER EIGHT

1. Under No Child Left Behind, AYP is the measure by which schools are judged. Schools that fail to make AYP for five years in a row are supposed to reinvent themselves into successful schools, a notion that proved to be fanciful.

2. These are the comprehensive high schools as opposed to the selective, specialty high schools.

3. Neither Rhee nor Cohen was familiar with Friends of Bedford. The original suggestion to consider the group came from a community activist involved with efforts to improve D.C.'s Coolidge High School.

4. Friends of Bedford also took over Coolidge High School, a less troubled D.C. high school that also faced reconstitution.

5. Through union-bargained forced placement, still in effect at that time (prior to the new contract being approved in June 2010) those counselors had a right to be placed at other schools—the "dance of the lemons" common in many school districts.

6. At Coolidge High School the new football coach was Natalie Randolph, who instantly drew national publicity as the nation's first female high school football coach.

7. "D.C. Public School Student-Athletes Struggle to Be Eligible for College Sports," Alan Goldenbach, *The Washington Post,* June 15, 2010.

8. "Dunbar High's Private Operator Is Dropped," Bill Turque, *The Washington Post*, Dec. 9, 2010.

9. Friends of Bedford remained in control of Coolidge High School.

CHAPTER NINE

1. Hardy's student body is 42 percent free and reduced-price lunch and 7 percent special education. Overall, D.C. schools are 66 percent free and reduced-price lunch and 19 percent special education. But you can't draw conclusions from the comparison, given the out-of-boundary enrollment process. Rhee believes Pope's student selection process was possibly discriminatory based on conversations between Pope and Abigail Smith, one of Rhee's top deputies.

2. Pope met for an interview he insisted be kept off the record. When I e-mailed him specific questions for

on-the-record responses, he denied his admissions process discriminated but declined to elaborate.

3. "Deciphering Schools Chancellor Michelle Rhee," Marc Fisher, *The Washington Post Magazine,* Sept. 27, 2009.

4. A process of trying to contact *Post* editors and writers individually from the editorial and Metro section led me to the *Post* spokesperson, who arranged an interview with Spayd. She agreed to take questions about all Rhee coverage issues.

5. A *Post* spokesperson submitted fifteen articles written about D.C. schools by several *Post* reporters in the thirteen months leading up to the September 2010 primary election (a time frame chosen by the *Post*) as evidence of school-based reporting. Other than two very good columns written by veteran *Post* education columnist Jay Mathews, I saw nothing to withdraw my observation: how would D.C. residents, on primary day, know what kind of job she was doing with the schools? The one exception was a profile of Sousa Middle School, which delved into the difficulties of turning around a failing urban middle school. In the end, however, the reporter failed to ask the obvious question: if the principal made these gains by replacing most of the existing staff, what does that say about the lack of progress at nearby schools that served the same kinds of students? Johnson Middle School, for example, started out as low as Sousa and never moved up. Is that because there were no radical staff turnovers at Johnson? Given the intense controversy in D.C. over teacher firings, a controversy that would rank as a top issue in the upcoming mayoral

primary, shouldn't the question have been asked? During my primary day interviewing, voters in Ward 7 repeatedly told me the teachers were dismissed for no apparent reason.

6. Turque, referring to his sometimes-rocky relationship with Rhee (at one point she refused to talk directly to him for nearly a year) says, "I think a lot of public officials, particularly those new to the public sector, get frustrated when they don't have complete control over the narrative, when they see that the daily coverage is not a seamless extension of their communications strategy."

7. "One Newspaper, Two Stories" Bill Turque, *The Washington Post,* Jan. 27, 2010.

8. Turque points to test score gains made under Janey, which he said raises the question of whether the Rhee gains were merely a continuation of a trend started by Janey.

9. In fairness, Janey lacked the considerable powers handed to Rhee by Fenty, who had seized control of the schools.

10. If Janey had education miracles up his sleeve, they never materialized in Newark, where he was in charge of schools longer than his D.C. tenure. In late summer 2010 the news broke that Janey would lose his Newark job.

11. In a second vote in November 2010, Baltimore teachers approved the contract.

12. "Rhee Needs to Look in the Mirror," Courtland Milloy, *The Washington Post,* Sept. 26, 2010.

13. "Is There Racism in Washington's School Reform?" *The Washington Post,* Oct. 2, 2010.

14. The layoffs were a mix of low performers and good teachers let go for other reasons, such as declining enrollments at a particular school or a decrease in the demand for the subject they taught. The complicated mix made it easy for Rhee opponents to identify a good teacher who had been laid off to hold up as an example of injustice.

15. Turque says the original DCPS statements about the firings were vague about which staffers were fired for which reasons. "It wasn't until sometime later that we had an exact number. . . . I think this is where things got lost in the fog of war."

16. Obtaining an exact racial breakdown on the layoffs and firings proved to be impossible. DCPS said those fired matched the overall demographic of the D.C. teacher corps. However, race is self-reported and optional. Many teachers decline to cite their race or ethnicity. It is safe to assume that the majority of D.C. teachers are black and therefore most of those fired were black.

CHAPTER TEN

1. On Nov. 2, 2010, Gray won the general election with more than 70 percent of the vote. His only real challenge came from write-in votes for Fenty, an effort seen as a pro-school reform statement.

2. Rhee resigned Oct. 13, roughly a month after Fenty's primary loss. "In short, we have

agreed—together—that the best way to keep the reforms going is for this reformer to step aside," said Rhee at a press conference as deputy chancellor, Kaya Henderson, was named interim chancellor.

3. In the 2010–2011 school year, there were 180 TFA corps members working in Washington. Roughly 40 percent were teachers of color; 17 percent were African American.

4. "Why Michelle Rhee's Education 'Brand' Failed in D.C.," Natalie Hopkinson, *The Atlantic,* Sept. 15, 2010.

5. Sample size around Sousa Middle School: 200. Margin of error: 6.9 percent. Interview dates: Sept. 22–25, 2010.

6. "How D.C. Mayor Fenty Lost the Black Vote—and His Job," Paul Schwartzman and Chris L. Jenkins, *The Washington Post,* Sept. 18, 2010.

7. Ibid.

8. "Fenty Says Education Reform Cost Him Re-Election," Mike Debonis, *The Washington Post.* Oct. 7, 2010.

9. "Teachers Union Helped Unseat Fenty," Ben Smith, *Politico,* Sept. 15, 2010.

10. Ibid.

11. Rhee and Johnson had intended to marry Sept. 4, 2010, in California, but postponed their vows, explaining in an e-mail: "The reason we are making this change is that our current wedding plans are not what we had intended. We underestimated the intensity of interest in the wedding and didn't manage that well, which was our responsibility."

12. Gray's staff turned down numerous requests for an interview.

CHAPTER ELEVEN

1. This exchange, including the quotes, comes from a case study session conducted by the MIT Sloan Management School. Janey declined to talk to me for this book. "Management Principles and the Washington, D.C. Public Schools." *MIT Sloan School of Management Case Study,* Sept. 7, 2010.

2. "Neglecting the Base," Bob Herbert, *The New York Times,* Sept. 20, 2010.

3. In fairness it should be noted that with four hundred thousand students Chicago Public Schools would be a far more difficult reform challenge.

4. The annual Broad Prize offers $2 million in student scholarships to the five finalist highest-performing urban districts, with the top winner receiving $1 million in prizes.

5. That estimate of one-third, which I use throughout the book, was drawn from interviews with experts both inside and outside D.C. schools. Based on my school visits, I found no reason to dispute it.

6. As of October 2010, DCPS records showed 2,318 teachers with a start date prior to June 2007 and 1,918 with a start date after that.

7. *Below C Level: How American Education Encourages Mediocrity and What We Can Do About It.* 2010.

8. This teacher originally agreed to talk for the record but later asked that her name be removed.

Chapter Twelve

1. "Census Estimate: D.C. Black Population Still Shrinking," Carol Morello, *The Washington Post,* Jan. 7, 2010.

2. In November 2010, after this chapter was written, Caruth was hired by DCPS's human resources department.

3. "Departing D.C. Schools Chancellor Michelle Rhee Offers Tough Advice in Tampa," Tom Marshall, *St. Petersburg Times,* Oct. 22, 2010.

4. I interviewed Johnson in November 2010.

5. "What I've Learned," Michelle Rhee, *Newsweek,* Dec. 6, 2010.

ABOUT THE AUTHOR

Richard Whitmire, a veteran newspaper reporter and editorial writer at *USA Today,* is the author of the recently published *Why Boys Fail,* which explores why boys are falling behind in K–12 schools. Whitmire worked on several upstate New York newspapers before coming to Washington, D.C., to be a national reporter for Gannett News Service (GNS) and to work on the design and launch of *USA Today.* After spending two years with *USA Today* he returned to GNS to cover the Pentagon. In 1986 he was a Knight Journalism Fellow at Stanford University, where he studied defense issues.

Later, Whitmire switched to the education beat and in 2000 he returned to *USA Today* to join the editorial page, where he wrote mostly about education issues. In 2008 he left the newspaper to focus on other education writing projects. In addition to the boys book he wrote numerous education commentaries that appeared in national publications including *The Washington Post, The Wall Street Journal, USA Today, Politico, U.S. News & World Report,* and *The New Republic.* In 2009 he served as the project journalist for the Broad Prize for Urban Education.

Whitmire lives in Arlington, Virginia, and is married to ABC News producer Robin Gradison. They have two daughters.

INDEX